CRIMINAL WOMEN
1850–1920

FAMILY HISTORY FROM PEN & SWORD

Tracing Secret Service Ancestors

Tracing Your Air Force Ancestors

Tracing Your Ancestors

Tracing Your Ancestors from 1066 to 1837

Tracing Your Ancestors Through Death Records

Tracing Your Ancestors Through Family Photographs

Tracing Your Ancestors Using the Census

Tracing Your Ancestors' Childhood

Tracing Your Ancestors' Parish Records

Tracing Your Aristocratic Ancestors

Tracing Your Army Ancestors – 2nd Edition

Tracing Your Birmingham Ancestors

Tracing Your Black Country Ancestors

Tracing Your British Indian Ancestors

Tracing Your Canal Ancestors

Tracing Your Channel Islands Ancestors

Tracing Your Coalmining Ancestors

Tracing Your Criminal Ancestors

Tracing Your East Anglian Ancestors

Tracing Your East End Ancestors

Tracing Your Edinburgh Ancestors

Tracing Your First World War Ancestors

Tracing Your Great War Ancestors: The Gallipoli Campaign

Tracing Your Great War Ancestors: The Somme

Tracing Your Great War Ancestors: Ypres

Tracing Your Huguenot Ancestors

Tracing Your Jewish Ancestors

Tracing Your Labour Movement Ancestors

Tracing Your Lancashire Ancestors

Tracing Your Leeds Ancestors

Tracing Your Legal Ancestors

Tracing Your Liverpool Ancestors

Tracing Your London Ancestors

Tracing Your Medical Ancestors

Tracing Your Merchant Navy Ancestors

Tracing Your Naval Ancestors

Tracing Your Northern Ancestors

Tracing Your Pauper Ancestors

Tracing Your Police Ancestors

Tracing Your Prisoner of War Ancestors: The First World War

Tracing Your Railway Ancestors

Tracing Your Royal Marine Ancestors

Tracing Your Rural Ancestors

Tracing Your Scottish Ancestors

Tracing Your Second World War Ancestors

Tracing Your Servant Ancestors

Tracing Your Service Women Ancestors

Tracing Your Shipbuilding Ancestors

Tracing Your Tank Ancestors

Tracing Your Textile Ancestors

Tracing Your Trade and Craftsmen Ancestors

Tracing Your Welsh Ancestors

Tracing Your West Country Ancestors

Tracing Your Yorkshire Ancestors

CRIMINAL WOMEN
1850–1920

*Researching the Lives of Female Criminals in
Britain and Australia*

Lucy Williams and Barry Godfrey

Pen & Sword
FAMILY HISTORY

First published in Great Britain in 2018 by
Pen & Sword Family History
an imprint of
Pen & Sword Books Ltd
47 Church Street
Barnsley
South Yorkshire
S70 2AS

ISBN 978 1 52671 861 7

A CIP catalogue record for this book is available from the British Library

Typeset in INDIA by Geniies IT & Services Private Limited

Printed and bound in (country) by CPI UK

Pen & Sword Books Ltd incorporates the imprints of Pen & Sword Archae-
ology, Atlas, Aviation, Battleground, Discovery, Family History, History,
Maritime, Military, Naval, Politics, Railways, Select, Social History, Transport, True Crime, and Claymore Press, Frontline Books, Leo Cooper, Prae-
torian Press, Remember When, Seaforth Publishing and Wharncliffe.

For a complete list of Pen & Sword titles please contact
PEN & SWORD BOOKS LIMITED
47 Church Street, Barnsley, South Yorkshire, S70 2AS, England
E-mail: enquiries@pen-and-sword.co.uk
Website: www.pen-and-sword.co.uk

CONTENTS

Part 1

BACKGROUND

Chapter 1

INTRODUCTION

Records of crime and disorder created by the British state between 1850 and 1925 are some of the most voluminous of all those available for the study of ordinary people in the last two centuries. However, while we might suppose that this would make the history of crime and criminals one of the easier histories to uncover, creating a criminal biography can leave us with a nasty shock. Unless you are tracing one of the handful of criminal celebrities in the nineteenth century, you may find this more difficult than you first imagine. People who broke the law usually had a vested interest in not being found. They used aliases, regularly changed addresses and weren't always the most truthful when officials asked them for details – information we rely on to find them and learn about their lives more than a century later. Female offenders can be amongst the hardest characters of all to find. Not only were they, like male offenders, keen to escape the eye of the authorities, but by virtue of being women, their identities were more changeable and their lives were less consistently recorded.

Family historians have long laboured to trace female relatives whose names might change at any time as they married, whose occupations were often ignored or misreported in civil records, and whose details might be left off vital household documents that were usually filled in by men. Those tracing criminal women will come across these same frustrating problems, and more besides. Female offenders might use professional aliases, or change their names on marriage, just like our other female ancestors, but they were also more likely than other groups of women to adopt new surnames at will, for example when in a long-term but not legally recognised relationship. Women might do this multiple times over the course of their adult lives. Criminal women might also be more likely than their 'stable' peers to have illegitimate children, whose births were never registered, and fathers never publicly acknowledged. From their early lives, women who ended up in the court dock may have regularly moved addresses, been passed around family members or been in and out of institutions around the country, leaving researchers scratching their heads in the attempt to piece together a credible journey.

Moreover, the dysfunctional lives that led many women into prisons, reformatories, transportation ships, lock hospitals and inebriates' homes also meant that the women we are looking for did not always have the clearest sense of their own details and histories. The women we find in these institutions might never have known the exact date and year of their birth, or may have had little cause to remember it in their adult lives. As such they might regularly misreport their age or place of birth by accident, giving changeable and conflicting estimates as they went through life. There were of course also those women who were intentionally vague about their details to census enumerators, courts and police officers in the hope of avoiding apprehension, identification, conviction or simply out of a sense of fun or mischief.

We are therefore often left in the position of tracing women who not only did not want to be found, and who, through little fault of their own, leave us with conflicting information about where and when they were born, how they made a living, or where we might find them. These women probably never anticipated that over a hundred years later we would be looking for them, eager to tell stories about their lives.

The lives of criminal women, however, remain some of the most intriguing, if least documented, stories of the last two centuries. The narratives of female offenders have the potential to challenge our perception of women in this era and to broaden our understanding of working-class lives. Such histories also have much to offer when it comes to expanding our knowledge of crime, disorder and the dark side of society in British history. The best part is that these histories are just waiting to be found. In this book, we provide our own collection of life histories of criminal women, and look at the documents and resources available to researchers for recovering these fascinating histories. We offer tips on where to look for the best criminal justice records, and also offer suggestions of how to make the most of well-known sources with tracing the lives of criminal women in mind. This book comprises three parts, and forty chapters, covering the context of crime and punishment in this era, colourful examples of criminal women's life narratives, and a 'how to' research guide for different collections.

In Chapters 2 to 5, we provide four background chapters on the history of women, crime and punishment. Each chapter provides an overview of an aspect of the research we aim to help readers carry out. These chapters also provide useful contextual information for Parts 2 and 3. The first chapter lists the most common crimes of property, violence and public order for which women were prosecuted. The second explores the range of, primarily institutional, punishments to which women in this period could be sentenced in court. As imprisonment was the central feature of the criminal justice system in our period, the third takes a closer look at the function and regime inside both local and convict prisons, while the fourth looks at how prisoners were released back into society, and how the state looked to keep them under surveillance post-sentence.

In Chapters 6 to 35 we provide life narratives of criminal women from across our period. Cases range from a few of the final women to be transported to Australia in the early 1850s, to a generation of young women incarcerated at the beginning of their lives in twentieth-century juvenile reformatories. By revealing these lives, we seek to convey not only the diversity of the crimes for which women were convicted, and the punishments they were subjected to, but also the different patterns that criminal activity could take in the female life-course – from young women whose later lives reflected nothing of their early transgressions, to women stuck in an almost life-long cycle of offending, imprisonment and reconviction. We hope that readers will find them to be informative and entertaining to read, and to take inspiration from our narratives to compile their own life histories of criminal women.

In Chapters 36 to 39 we focus on how to carry out research into different aspects of criminal lives. We discuss the key sources we used to compile our life histories, how to access them, and their benefits and pitfalls. We have chosen to focus on four areas of criminal women's stories, and tackle them in the order in which researchers usually find them. First, women and crime, exploring the records available to find out more about crimes themselves; second, women and imprisonment, for those wishing to further their understanding of the emotional and physical realities of punishment in this prison; third, the state's records on criminal women during imprisonment and after release; and lastly, the broader lives of criminal women, and the civil records that can tell us more about their circumstances outside the courtroom or prison. The final chapter concludes our book and we point towards some further reading that might help or inform people who want to take their research a step further.

However, first we turn to women's involvement in crime, and delve into the history of these fascinating characters, their punishments and the systems that sought to keep them in check.

Chapter 2

WOMEN AND CRIME

W hen we think of criminals between 1850 and 1925 we might imagine the spectral figure of 'Jack the Ripper' lurking in Whitechapel alleyways, or perhaps the 'Artful Dodger' picking pockets in a crowded public place. We might think of the most famous murders of the day, or the petty crimes that kept policemen pacing the beat; and travellers in Britain's towns and cities keeping a watchful eye on their wallets. Women, however, do not normally spring to mind.

Histories of the nineteenth and early twentieth centuries, and our Victorian forebears themselves, have encouraged us to think of women in particular ways – the fancy ladies in the latest fashions, the domestic angel tending hearth and home, or perhaps even the weary working woman, spending long hours at the factory or obediently cleaning their master and mistress's home. Women in the past, from our grandmothers to our great-great-great grandmothers, we are told, were gentle, domestic, morally upstanding, chaste and well behaved. At least, they were supposed to be. While it is true that the majority of women between 1850 and 1925 led perfectly ordinary, more-or-less law-abiding, lives, a substantial minority were challenging assumptions and expectations about women in their period, and continue to challenge our understanding of them today. Among the Dickens-worthy cast of male thieves, swindlers and murderers that could be found on Britain's streets, there were female faces too – women every bit as capable of deception, violence and disorder as their male counterparts.

Throughout our period, women broke the law and faced the consequences just like male offenders, although their journeys to and through the criminal justice system were often subtly different.

There was considerable overlap between the crimes of men and women in this period, but women also carried out a range of offences specific to their identities, skills and circumstances. When convicted, female offenders to a large extent faced the same range of sentences and punishments as men, though by the mid-nineteenth century onwards they had their own penal institutions. In cases of particularly female offences, such as prostitution, women had laws and institutions designed specifically for them (as was the case of Elizabeth Coppin, see Chapter 29). The periods of life in which they found themselves caught up with crime and patterns of offending could be different too.

Though men made up the majority of those convicted and imprisoned in this period, women were more vulnerable to repeat offending, known as recidivism, and extreme recidivism at that. While men were more likely to be prosecuted for crime, women who broke the law were more likely to do so again and again. Some female offenders could amass more than a hundred convictions in just a few years. The most extreme could commit hundreds over a lifetime.

Women were in some ways more socially vulnerable than men to offending in the first place. Their opportunities for employment were already more limited and more poorly paid than men's. The majority of women who ended up in the criminal justice system were working-class women, and poverty played a large role in crimes of theft, public order and even violence. Life crises, such as the birth of an illegitimate child, or loss of a family breadwinner, also fell more heavily on women. In many cases women were more dependent on the financial and social support of others than their male contemporaries, who maintained the opportunity to operate freely in society (at least in theory).

The cultural gender expectations of the day similarly played an important role in women's recidivism. While a man could be convicted of violence, or drunk and disorderly behaviour', yet still adhere to common notions of masculinity, a violent, drunken or sexually 'aggressive' woman (like a prostitute) dramatically challenged the idea of femininity. In doing so she flouted social expectation, and challenged authority in more ways than one. A woman's first conviction would tarnish her reputation, some historians have argued irrevocably. Female offenders in many instances were conceptualised as those who had not only flouted the criminal law, but also the moral laws of society – a criminal woman was a 'bad' woman in more ways than one. A tarnished character, or a reputation as a disorderly, immoral or subversive woman might prohibit an individual from finding work, maintaining stable relationships with partners, family and neighbours, or even finding appropriate accommodation. These factors each contributed to women's offending in the first place and certainly heightened the likelihood of them offending over and again. A significant proportion of offending women, like Elizabeth Dillon (see Chapter 15) and Ann Plowman (see Chapter 28), could find themselves stuck in an impossible cycle of crime, social exclusion, diminished options and reoffending.

Most convictions of women in this period would take place at local magistrates' courts, also called police courts. These courts heard cases daily and gave magistrates the power to impose fines, dismiss and discharge cases with little or conflicting evidence, and impose short sentences of imprisonment for crimes of violence, property and public order. For crimes obviously more serious in nature (for example, murder, manslaughter or thefts of large sums) or when dealing with a serious recidivist, magistrates would refer cases to the higher courts, known as assizes or sessions. These courts sat at less regular intervals, and might leave offenders waiting several weeks for a day in court. Trials at the sessions were held by a judge and jury and had the ability to impose much lengthier sentences of imprisonment, and even the death sentence.

Before we can consider what happened to women when they offended and how we might trace them, we must first know more about how women broke the law, and what their crimes looked like. The offences for which men and women were convicted were largely the same (although the proportion of convictions could differ significantly according to gender). The only convictions we don't commonly find against women in this period include sexual offences (apart from bigamy), treason or so-called white-collar crimes such as embezzlement.

The following pages give a brief overview of the three main categories of crime which women committed (and still do today): property, violence and public order.

PROPERTY OFFENCES

Until the second half of the twentieth century, the law still tended to place heavier penalties on crimes against property than those against individuals. Women's crimes against property far outweighed their crimes of violence, and were the offences most likely to see them prosecuted in higher courts and transported to Australia or sent for a spell of penal servitude in convict prison. Although most of the property crimes women carried out, whether petty larceny (thefts of small value) or felony larceny (thefts perceived more serious in nature or higher value), were essentially the acquisition of items and money that did not belong to them, there was an astonishing range of ways in which theft was carried out.

Larceny from the person, or simply pocket picking, was perhaps the most common of all women's property offences. Shops, pubs, crowded streets and market places all provided ample opportunity for the light-fingered to make away with small but valuable items. However, there was more than one way to steal from the person. Offences ranged from prostitutes who robbed inebriated (or in extreme cases drugged) customers as they slept, to women who lured young children into alleyways and stripped them of anything of value – on some occasions even their clothes.

The crime of *robbery with violence* was an extension of larceny from the person and was essentially any theft from a person where physical force was used, where the victim was injured or sometimes even simply considered themselves in danger. These could range from a tussle on the street between a pickpocket and a victim who had caught them in the act, to more serious violence like the rash of garrotting that took place in the 1860s, or even the occasional death at the hands of a thief, like the offence Mary Fitzpatrick may or may not have been guilty of (see Chapter 32).

For all the risk of theft on the street, the home was by no means a safe place for property. Many younger women who appeared in court were placed on trial for the crime of *theft by a servant*, a largely self-explanatory crime which saw domestic servants steal money, jewellery, clothing, material, cutlery and even furniture from their employers. These offences lacked the immediate crisis of poverty often evident in other property crimes (female domestic servants up until the First World War commonly received a small wage and bed and board from their employers), yet for young women paid very low wages, the wealth and opulence they spent their days surrounded by were often difficult to resist. Ordinary homes were vulnerable too. In an age before security systems, where doors might commonly be left unlocked and regularly changing residents meant unfamiliar faces never looked out of place, the homes of average working families could be a thief's paradise. *Burglary* and *housebreaking* could provide women with easy access to everyday household items to keep or sell.

Shoplifting was also a common crime by women during our period. While we might think of light-fingered ladies stowing perfumes from high-class boutiques in their petticoats, this was a crime most often carried out by working-class women in ordinary neighbourhood shops. Small items that could be stowed under large dresses, in pockets or up sleeves were preferable, but women would also commonly steal yards of fabric and large quantities of fresh produce. Towards the end of our period, in the post-war years and early 1920s, department stores were on the rise and a new style of shoplifting developed. Larger stores with a range of goods displayed within easy reach instead of behind the counter changed the nature of goods that shoplifters were able to make away with, the value of items they could procure and the regularity with which they could ply their trade. Girl shoplifting gangs, most famously London's Forty Elephants, could undertake shoplifting on an industrial scale and for a short time were decried as the scourge of law and order. Dresses, shoes, fur coats and silk camisoles all became items of demand, and easy pickings for thieves. In the early twentieth century shoplifting became one of the easiest ways for female thieves to enjoy the latest fashions, and to turn a profit on the side.

There were of course also offences relating to disposing of stolen goods, as well as taking them. There were two prominent kinds of prosecution for this offence. The first was for *receiving stolen goods* – prosecutions against women (usually older women) who bought stolen goods cheaply and sold them on as market sellers or street vendors. The second was for *feloniously pawning*. While pawn shops offered a legitimate way for thousands of struggling families to raise extra cash in times of need, or bridge shortfalls in the household budget until payday, they were also a very convenient way for offenders to trade stolen goods for cash. Items could be pledged at a pawnshop, usually less scrupulous establishments that cared little for the provenance of items, and the offender could leave quickly with cash. It was the quickest and easiest way to dispose of stolen goods, especially for those who had no intention of redeeming the item and so destroyed the collection ticket, and with it the only remaining evidence of their crime.

A small number of women in this period would find themselves prosecuted for *fraud* and *forgery*. These were blanket terms used to describe a broad range of offences that required a greater use of deception than ordinary thefts. Crimes might range from forging large bank notes or payment orders, eliciting donations from charities or individuals under false pretences, attempting to defraud insurance companies with false claims or damage to property (*arson* was often a tactic used by those wishing to make insurance claims). Though the (relatively common) crime of *production and distribution of counterfeit coins* was, in practice, a kind of forgery, any offence relating to counterfeit coins was actually tried as a *'Royal Offence'*, a crime against the crown. Due to the widespread and persistent nature of making bad coins and introducing them into circulation, women convicted of coining offences, like Eleanor Boniface (see Chapter 10), would usually face a large term of imprisonment.

VIOLENT OFFENCES

Despite the domestic ideals held up to them by society, very few women managed to spend their entire lives as passive, fragile creatures who knew little of life but hearth and home. For some women, life turned out to be a much harder and more physically violent existence than the feminine ideals of the day might lead one to believe. Women could fight every inch as bitterly, and act in violence just as desperately, as their male counterparts.

Some of the saddest and most commonly publicised incidents of female violence are those that occurred against children. *Infanticide* was the term used to describe the killing of young children (commonly those up to about 3 or 4 years of age), usually by their mother. Infanticide might occur directly after birth as the desperate mothers of illegitimate children sought a way to hide the outcome of an unplanned (or in some cases unnoticed) pregnancy. Infanticide might also happen to older children too, as mothers failed to live with the social ostracism illegitimate children could cause, or struggled to cope financially. Although those who committed infanticide were prosecuted for the crime, the law was not blind to the plight of unwed and desperate mothers. Sympathy for their circumstances and a growing awareness of mental health meant that mothers found guilty of infanticide might only serve short terms of imprisonment (one or two years in a convict prison) or, as the period wore on, find themselves placed in a more supportive and therapeutic environment than a prison – such was the case of Ann Nicholls (see Chapter 9).

Conversely, however, child murder when carried out by a woman other than the mother was met with significant social outrage, and those responsible could expect to face the strongest punishments the law had available. No female offender was more hated than the figure of the babyfarmer. *Babyfarming* was the practice of commercialised childcare in which a woman (or sometimes two working together) would take into their care young children whom parents were struggling to care for. Many of these children were the illegitimate offspring of young unwed mothers. Babyfarmers would charge a one-off payment for an 'adoption' of the child, or accept weekly maintenance payments from parents intending to one day reclaim their children. Whilst this practice in itself was not illegal, in many cases, the majority of money received from parents was not spent on children. It was not uncommon for babyfarmers to care for five or ten children simultaneously, many of whom met with abuse, neglect or death from violence, drugging or starvation. Babyfarmers like Amelia Sach (see Chapter 6) when caught would face a hostile courtroom and the full brunt of the law. They were some of the only criminal women still being hanged by the end of the nineteenth century.

Later in the nineteenth century, particularly after the formation of local societies and then the National Society for the Prevention of Cruelty to Children in 1884, prosecutions for child neglect and abuse began to increase. Prior to this time, whilst serious cases of abuse violence against children did come to courts, parents and guardians were largely left alone by the state to care for and discipline their children as they saw fit. Women, as the parent or guardian likely to be responsible for domestic life and childcare, were also most likely to be prosecuted for parental *neglect*. While not always premeditated or intentional, as the twentieth century dawned, the abuse and neglect of children was treated increasingly seriously, as we can see in the case of Maria Dibsdale (see Chapter 31).

However, for all the press attention given to tragic cases of infanticide, or the public outcry over babyfarming, the majority of violent crimes women carried out were against other adults. *Murders* or *manslaughters* committed by women made some of the most famous court cases of the age. From Florence Maybrick, whose potential miscarriage of justice has been immortalised on page and stage, to the serial killer Catherine Wilson, who became the last woman to be publicly executed in England, the female murderer became the antithesis of all society expected from women. However, cases of female murder or manslaughter were not common. When they did occur, they were usually against family members (parents, siblings, aunts and uncles) or partners, less often from poisoning or cold-blooded planning, than from spontaneous violence in the heat of a fight or row. Fatal crime by women was in many respects the most serious outcome of *domestic violence*, one of the hardest crimes to trace on account of both the hidden nature of violence in the home, and male victims' reticence to report assaults by women.

The most common crimes of violence which came daily through the courts were women's violent crimes against other women.

In cramped housing and crowded streets where resources were scarce and feuds easily created, tempers could flare and bubble easily over into violence. Women *fighting* between themselves, and their *assaults* on each other over matters of the heart, money, insults given and received, and ownership of items, could be as minor as pulling hair and pushing and shoving or involve using weapons, drawing blood and endangering life.

PUBLIC ORDER OFFENCES

Women were far more likely to commit lower level crimes which breached laws concerning public order than they were to commit crimes of theft and serious violence. Offences against public order and decency came in many forms, and saw women sentenced at local magistrates' courts to fines or short terms of imprisonment that could last anywhere from a few days to weeks or months in prison.

Prostitution is one of the most famous female offences in the world, and has been since records of crime began. Trading sex for money was not illegal during our period. However, this does not mean that prostitution was in anyway condoned or approved by the British state, or by British society. The police and courts had a number of ways in which they could prosecute women working as prostitutes, punishing their behaviour, and keeping them (albeit for short periods of time) off the streets.

Women working as prostitutes might be prosecuted for *public obscenity*, or the use of *obscene language*. The remit of this offence was broad, and women might be prosecuted under it for something as minor as using graphic language too loudly in the street, or abusing a police officer who tried to move them on, or it might be the result of conducting a sex act in public, or exposing themselves as they attempted to solicit customers. Public urination could also count as public obscenity, though was rarely used against otherwise 'law-abiding' members of the public.

Prostitutes might also be arrested simply for *causing a public nuisance*. The nuisance might constitute making too much noise, shouting and laughing, or it might mean harassment of members of the public who were travelling through or operating in the area. Offending a 'respectable' gentleman by propositioning him as he walked by might be enough to gain arrest for causing a nuisance if he decided to complain to a constable. The same event might also find a women prosecuted for *obstructing a public thoroughfare*.

As prostitutes aged, they might be given the opportunity to earn money by enticing or tricking new girls and young women into the trade. These women were known as procuresses. Convictions for *procuring* other women to work as prostitutes were rare, much rarer than the prevalence of the practice might suggest. However, trial rates could spike during times of national anxiety or local social concern about prostitution. The most famous of these was in England (London, particularly) during the 1880s following the publication of William Stead's *The Maiden Tribute of Modern Babylon,* in which the trade in child prostitutes in the capital was exposed. The Contagious Diseases Acts of 1866–86 similarly cast negative attention on all those working in the sex trade. Just like the prostitutes they sourced or housed, those supporting the trade, procuresses and brothel owners were often prosecuted under tangential public order legislation, rather than explicitly the activities they were carrying out. Madams who kept prostitutes, profited from their earnings and lured women into the trade might be prosecuted for *'living from immoral earnings'*, *'keeping a disorderly house'* or *'running a house of ill-fame'*. Where this was not possible, the authorities might attempt to prosecute them under licensing provisions for selling alcohol, or allowing illegal gambling in their establishment.

Prostitutes were not the only women arrested for breaches of public order. Perhaps the biggest categories of public order offence, *drunkenness* and *disorderly conduct*, could apply to any women in a public space (though there was a special category for female sex-workers, that of *'disorderly prostitute'*). Like other public order offences drunkenness and disorderly conduct covered a range of behaviours and could be used together to constitute a single offence (i.e. drunk and disorderly) or separately. Being drunk was not a crime, but drunken behaviour could be. Women who imbibed too much and could no longer take care of themselves could be prosecuted as *drunk and incapable*, and the shouting, quarrels and dangerous behaviour that accompanied low inhibitions could be prosecuted as *disorder*.

Only one kind of property crime was solely dealt with at the lower courts, and that was *criminal damage*. The majority of the prosecutions for criminal damage were for breaking windows, either by accident or on purpose. Throwing bricks and stones could be resort of disgruntled pub customers or quarrelling neighbours. Criminal damage might also be prosecuted under the offence of *riotous behaviour*, which was usually a combination of disorderly behaviour and criminal damage.

This brief overview is by no means comprehensive. Rather, it sets out the main categories of offence for which women were commonly prosecuted. Women will have had ways of making money, breaking the rules and settling scores for which they were never caught, and which have now, a hundred years later, slipped from memory and from record. Those crimes we know about are the ones that have been handed down to us, from early social investigators who anxiously chronicled crime in the towns and cities of Britain, from court reports and prison documents, and in some rare cases from the testimony of offenders themselves. Although these sources would often have us believe that being apprehended for a crime or facing the courtroom was the end of an offender's story, in many cases it was just the close of the first chapter in a fascinating journey that took them through the criminal justice system and out the other side again. In the next chapters, we look at the wide range of sentences used to punish and control criminal women, and offer some brief information, for intrepid researchers, on where they might be found after they left the courtroom.

Chapter 3

WOMEN AND PUNISHMENT

The British criminal justice system and women's place within it was in a state of flux in 1850. Previous decades had seen the decline of the 'bloody code' – a form of punishment in the eighteenth and early nineteenth century in which floggings, brandings, whippings and hangings were popular forms of justice used to punish the body, and were designed to act as a deterrent to spectators who watched the punishment take place. By the mid-century, imprisonment was becoming the main form of punishment in the United Kingdom, although older systems like convict transportation to Australia were not yet dispensed with. Likewise, while women in centuries past had been able to rely on legal loopholes such as 'femme covert' (the idea that a woman, under the control of her husband, could not truly be held responsible for her criminal actions) and the chivalry of the courtroom to avoid punishment, times were changing. As ideas about femininity, gender and crime all changed, so did women's experiences of justice. Here, we briefly explore the range of punishments that might await women who broke the law.

BEYOND THE SEAS

The history of convict transportation stretches back far longer than the nineteenth century. Criminal women from the seventeenth century onwards might find themselves packed aboard a ship and sent to the American colonies as indentured servants, and a century later to the west coast of Africa, where many faced disease, starvation and death. However, from 1787 Australia became the main penal colony for the disposal of unruly women.

From the early nineteenth century until the end of penal transportation for women in 1853 (a further 10,000 male convicts would face transportation to a new penal colony in Western Australia before the end of transportation to Australia in 1868) Van Diemen's Land, a lush green island off the southern coast of Australia, was the primary destination for convicts. For the first three years of our period, transportation was still a popular punishment for women convicted of felony (more serious) offences. After sentencing at court, women would be transferred to a holding prison (usually Millbank), where they would wait to be loaded onto a convict vessel. However, once sentenced to transportation, arrival in Australia was by no means assured. Whether women were young, healthy and able-bodied enough, if their sentences met the desired criteria or if they happened to be in the right location as a convict ship came in, could all be important factors in making it on board a convict vessel. While there were hundreds of women sentenced to transportation across the seas between 1850 and 1853, many initially sentenced to transportation remained in Britain when they were imprisoned, pardoned, had their sentences reduced or were left behind being for being pregnant, too old or too infirm.

The final female convict ship, carrying 220 women, was the *Duchess of Northumberland*. The ship left Britain in November 1852 and arrived in Van Diemen's Land the following April. Shipwrecks were rare, and almost all convict vessels made it safely to Australia. However, well-being on board was not guaranteed. Although by the 1850s every care was taken to ensure healthy convicts arrived in the colonies, sudden illness or a difficult pregnancy or birth could strike at any time, and left transported women vulnerable to death before their sentences had even begun.

On arrival in Van Diemen's land, women at the end of the convict period would have been assigned to work as servants in private households (not dissimilar to the experience of women in colonial America a century before), or, if found to be too unruly, they could be sent to one of the 'female factories'. The factories operated much like English local prisons, where women would be incarcerated and expected to carry out daily labour. A transported woman in the

1850s could typically expect to be granted a 'ticket-of-leave' half way through her sentence, providing their conduct under sentence had been good. A ticket-of-leave entitled them to conditional freedom in the colony. Providing they adhered to the strict conditions attached to their liberty until the rest of their sentence expired, female convicts would be free to undertake paid employment, to marry and to live outside the convict establishment. Once the term of their sentence expired, women were free to return to Britain (though very few did) or to live out their lives in Australia as colonial citizens.

After the end of penal transportation to Van Diemen's Land, (which became known as Tasmania in 1856 in an attempt to shake off its penal colony past) any convicts under sentence continued to serve their time until they had worked their way through the convict system and obtained liberty. Although Tasmania ceased to be a penal settlement in the 1850s, that did not mean an end to crime in the colony nor the need for the penal establishment put in place by the British. Ex-convicts, the children of convicts and free settlers alike continued to break the law, and information on their lives and crimes in the late nineteenth and early twentieth centuries can be found in the very same criminal justice records established by the convict system that came before.

ALBION'S FATAL TREE

Capital punishment operated throughout the nineteenth century, and continued for women up until the last female convict, Ruth Ellis, was hanged for the murder of her lover in 1955 (capital punishment was abolished for England and Wales ten years later in 1965). However, by the early twentieth century, it was highly unusual for women to face a capital sentence, with just a few executions of women occurring each decade.

For women, capital punishment was also a last resort in the second half of the nineteenth century. While judges would often don the traditional black cap, and pronounce a sentence of death upon individuals who had committed murder or serious assaults, these were, more-often-than-not, commuted to a sentence of life imprisonment after the defendant or her sympathisers successfully petitioned the Queen or the Secretary of State.

Between 1850 and 1868, those women unlucky enough to have their capital sentences carried out would have suffered a public execution. These well-attended events, intended to act as a deterrent to spectators and convey a powerful message about the might of the law, could draw in thousands of people from the local area and further abroad. At a public execution there might be street vendors selling food or refreshments, street-entertainers, public speakers and there would be opportunities to pick up souvenir programmes (called broadsides). A crowd could gather hours before the execution, and strain to get a glimpse of the condemned as they were led out onto especially erected gallows, and see justice was dispensed.

Frances Kidder became the last women to be publicly hanged in Britain when she was executed at midday outside the main gate of Maidstone prison on 2 April 1868 for the murder of her 10-year-old stepdaughter. The Capital Punishment Amendment Act of May 1868 put an end to public execution; after this, capital convicts had to be executed inside the walls of the prison in which they were being held. For almost another hundred years, executions would be carried out with only a few official spectators (medical officer, religious official, governor of the prison).

Between 1850 and 1925 the hanging of women was not common. There was a social and cultural aversion to hanging women, due to both the harrowing physical reality of doing so, and the contrast of brutal physical punishment with contemporary ideas about gender. Throughout this period, execution was usually reserved for women who had committed what were perceived to be the most heinous offences – crimes of passion where spouses, lovers or lovers' wives were murdered, or the murder of children for gain, such as in the case of notorious 'babyfarmers' Amelia Sach and Margaret Walters (see Chapter 6).

IMPRISONMENT

From 1853, when the Transportation Bill supplemented penal servitude abroad (transportation) for terms of penal servitude at home, the fate of criminal women in Britain was irrevocably changed. From 1853, women could no longer be placed out of the sight and mind of the British authorities in Australia, and had to be imprisoned in England. A few large prisons and a number of small lock-ups had existed before the 1850s, but until the first few decades of the nineteenth century, prisons functioned more as holding pens for those awaiting trial or another punishment than as the punishment itself. Until the mid-nineteenth century, it was highly unusual for a sentence of imprisonment to extend past two years as there was neither the space nor facilities to deal with prisoners over the longer term. Those convicted of more serious crimes would face the gallows or penal transportation rather than life inside a cell. However, changing sensibilities to capital sentences (especially for women) and the evolving needs of Britain's overseas colonies necessitated a more modern penal solution. The first of England's great convict prisons was Millbank, built on the side of the Thames between 1812 and 1821, admitting its first female prisoners in 1816 (and men from 1817). It was here that the idea of offering terms of imprisonment instead of transportation began. However, it was only with the establishment of other institutions, most notably Pentonville in 1842 and Dartmoor as a civilian prison in 1851, that the modern prison as a place of reform and redemption, as well as punishment, became a mainstay of British justice.

There were two types of imprisonment that female offenders might experience. The first and most common kind was at the local level. Small prisons, borough and county gaols, lock-ups, houses of detention and correction all confined disorderly women. These institutions catered for those serving anywhere from a few days to two years in prison. After the disastrous and dangerous mixed prisons of the eighteenth century, nineteenth-century houses of detention either had entirely separate institutions for men and women or, at the very least, separate wings. In local prisons women were not subject to the same hard physical labour as men.

From 1853 those women found guilty of felony offences would usually undertake a term of penal servitude. Sentences of penal servitude ranged anywhere from three years to life in prison. Penal servitude was significantly different from imprisonment at the local level. Upon entry convicts were stripped of the trappings of their former lives. Their hair was cut, they were placed in a convict uniform, and processed into the prison. For a large part of our period, the first nine months of any sentence would be passed in the separate and silent system, a period where women were inducted into the strict regime of daily prison life (see Chapter 3). After this, women would progress into the central prison system, and spend their days undertaking prison labour such as knitting and sewing, or work in the prison laundry or kitchens. The intention of the convict system was not only to remove female offenders from the circumstances, environments, and communities in which they offended (until the early twentieth century all of Britain's convict prisons were based in London), but also to change their character, using a strict routine and regular punishment to rebuild them as moral, law-abiding women.

FINES, SURETIES, ADMONISHMENTS AND DISCHARGES

Not all crimes ended with the loss of liberty. There were so many ways for women to violate the law that it was simply not practical to make every offence liable to imprisonment or transportation. For many offences that threatened public order – drunkenness, obscenity, disorderly conduct and for low-level violence resulting from family quarrels – magistrates might simply admonish and discharge offenders, warning them not to misbehave again, impose a small fine for the offence or request a monetary guarantee (a surety) for future good behaviour. These financial punishments were intended to have a deterrent effect on petty offenders, making minor public order infractions simply 'not worth' the cost of punishment. Sureties could be large financial sums (typically £5–£40) which an offender was required to provide to ensure good behaviour for a certain time. For example, a woman convicted of a violent quarrel with a neighbour might be required to provide £5 sureties and bound over to 'keep the peace' for six months. Providing she did not offend again during this time, at the end of the period the money would be returned to her. However, if she committed another offence against public order in this time, the money would be kept by the criminal justice system.

Fines were issued as punishments for crimes like drunk and disorderly behaviour or the use of obscene language. These fines, usually at a few shillings a time, were a punishment for, and deterrent against, those who caused a public nuisance. Fines might also incorporate the cost of criminal damage to property (like broken windows or glasses in a pub) and the court might also impose a similar financial penalty in the way of 'costs', intended to help to cover the enormous financial burden of administering a criminal justice system in which thousands of petty offences were heard by magistrates every week. However, when a fine was not, or could not be, paid, offenders could find themselves imprisoned for a few days or up to a month instead. While there was logic in imposing fines for crimes that were not severe or significant enough to warrant imprisonment, in many cases this only served to intensify the poverty that contributed to the crimes they sought to eradicate. Many women, such as Ann Plowman (see Chapter 28) found themselves taking to the streets to earn money to pay fines, yet in doing so became further embroiled in behaviour that brought them back to court.

ALTERNATIVE INSTITUTIONS

As the nineteenth century wore on, an ever more diverse collection of institutions developed to deal with female deviancy. The justice system used these institutions to separate out old offenders from juvenile delinquents, hardened offenders from habitual drunks, and the morally deviant from the criminally insane. Outside of transportation and imprisonment, there are several other forms of punishment imposed on offending women.

Reformatory Schools

The middle of the nineteenth century wasn't just a time when ideas were changing about gender, and about crime and punishment. From 1850 onwards, social understandings of the entire life-cycle were adapting. It was during this period that society started to recognise the special developmental and psychological significance of early life. The Victorians were the first to understand the unique developmental stage of childhood, and to legislate for it. The same developments that saw the nineteenth century bring in compulsory schooling for children, limited the type and hours of work they could undertake, and the advent of the National Society for the Prevention of Cruelty to Children, also saw a host of new institutions created for their care and control.

Reformatory schools were created in the 1860s specifically to deal with the problem of juvenile offenders. Whereas previously children who broke the law had been subject to the same processes and punishments as adult offenders, by the mid-nineteenth century the authorities recognised the problems caused by allowing young and vulnerable children (often guilty only of petty theft and disorder) to mix with hardened offenders. From the 1860s, magistrates had the power to send children for a short term of imprisonment (it was thought that seven to twenty-eight days would give children the short, sharp shock of adult prison life, without traumatising or corrupting them with a long sentence) and then to three to seven years in a reformatory. Children, like Eva Bebbington (see Chapter 16) and Elizabeth Coppin (see Chapter 29), classified as being at risk of becoming adult criminals, could be kept in a reformatory school until they were 16 or 18 years of age. The aim of the reformatory school was threefold. First, they removed vulnerable children from the homes, neighbourhoods and associations thought to draw them into crime. Second, the regime of the institution focused on strong religious education and moral discipline, in which children would be taught to be honest, well behaved and industrious. Third, the reformatories tried to train children for future employment – thought to be key for a stable law-abiding adult life. For reformatory girls, this meant training them thoroughly in domestic duties so that they might find work as servants or laundresses. Provision for juvenile offenders grew throughout our period, and by the early twentieth century, juvenile offenders even had their own courts.

Inebriate Reformatories

Drunkenness and the disorderly behaviour it caused were some of the most common offences amongst women in the nineteenth century. Developments in psychology and criminology in the latter decades of the century saw experts searching for explanations of how and why the abuse of alcohol occurred, and the solution to it. Theories surrounding hereditary weakness to alcohol abuse, and, for the first time, the disease of alcoholism, saw the state look for new ways to tackle this costly and anti-social offence.

The Habitual Drunkards Act of 1879 had enabled residential treatment as an alternative to prison, although its cost was prohibitive for many poor and working-class women. The 1898 Inebriates Act empowered local councils to establish and administer certified inebriate reformatories which were paid for by central government, local authorities and charitable donations. The 1902 Licensing Act established new systems for prohibiting the sale of alcohol to known drunkards, and barred many from licensed premises. Under the Act, habitual drunks attempting to purchase alcohol, and landlords who served them, could both be prosecuted. By the turn of the twentieth century, those prosecuted under the Acts could not just be fined or sent to prison, they could be required to undergo confinement in a certified inebriate reformatory, or home for the criminally inebriate, for a period of up to three years.

In such institutions women (a very high proportion of places at inebriate institutions were reserved for women who, supposed weak-minded, were felt to be particularly susceptible to overindulging in the demon drink) were kept under strict medical observation and educated in the benefits of a moral, sober and industrious life. Inside the institution, much like children in reformatories, female inebriates such as Amelia Layton (see Chapter 27) and Maria Dibsdale (see Chapter 31) were kept away from the environments and company in which they drank, and from alcohol itself, treated for any withdrawal symptoms and encouraged to learn skills that would help them find employment and productive lives upon release. When discharged from the inebriate home, women would often be supervised, much in the way of modern probation, to ensure that they did not return to their previous habits, as well as supported by medical professionals for up to a year.

Broadmoor Criminal Lunatic Asylum

In 1863, the first institution designed specifically for the care of criminal lunatics was established in England (Mary Ann Parr, see Chapter 19, was the first woman sent there). Broadmoor Hospital in Berkshire provided a secure, therapeutic, penal environment for two types of offenders.

The first were those, like Sarah Chiswell (see Chapter 23), found unfit to stand trial, or tried and found not guilty by way of insanity, who were termed 'Queen's Lunatics' and transferred directly to Broadmoor where they were held at her Majesty's pleasure until the medical officer informed the Secretary of State that they were safe to be released.

There were also criminal lunatics, who had been found guilty of felony offences and begun their sentences in convict prison only to be declared insane during their sentence. Convicts could then be transferred to Broadmoor. If, when re-evaluated on a yearly basis, the convict was found to be sane, they could be transferred back to convict prison. At the end of their sentence, a convict lunatic, if evaluated to be sane, could be released just as if they had been in prison.

Broadmoor's female inmates have been remarkably under-researched, but the crimes for which they were incarcerated were usually severe. Infanticide, murder and manslaughter were all common offences amongst female 'Queen's Lunatics', particularly those who had killed their children in a puerperal mania (what we would now call post-natal depression). The criminal lunatics were often those who had exhibited very disorderly behaviour in convict prisons, and who may have already had long criminal careers involving theft and public disorder. Broadmoor's regime was substantially different from the convict system, with a higher staff to inmate ratio, a more domestic setting and an emphasis on therapeutic treatment. Although it catered for both men and women, the more therapeutic environment suited many of the women who had been sent there for committing infanticide during episodes of mental instability.

CONCLUSION

From 1850, the British state developed more ways than ever before to tackle and confine women society considered 'deviant' – from reformatory schools for the youngest wayward girls, and special institutions for the mentally ill or those battling addiction, to convict prisons for the most serious offenders. In the next chapters, we take a look at what daily life was like for women who ended up behind bars, and what lay in store for them when they were released back onto the streets again.

Chapter 4

WOMEN IN THE PRISON SYSTEM

As the previous chapters have shown, most women in the nineteenth century were prosecuted for minor offences which attracted fines or short periods in gaol. Their time inside prison was short, usually less than six months, and they then quickly came out to be reunited with their families, their friends and their social situations. Many of the discharged women soon returned to local prisons, spending large parts of their lives revolving between prison and home life. The vast majority of the women who were convicted served their many short sentences in local prisons.

The governance, regime and funding of local prisons were all controlled at a county level, and consequently there was a considerable amount of variation in the local prison system. Some counties were not willing to invest in prison buildings when times were hard, or even when times were good. There was little point in investing in reformative infrastructure in any case, with so many women passing in and out on a daily basis, and the time and efforts of prison staff largely taken up with administration of reception, discharge and daily running requirements. It was alleged that local prisons were not only incapable of reforming female 'regulars' who knew the ropes, women who could easily spend a few months away family and for whom the shock of imprisonment was not great; the local prison was also seen by some women as refuge from squalid housing conditions and violent partners, a place preferable to home life or other state institutions, as was the case of Ann Plowman (see Chapter 28). Whilst this may seem like the 'prison holiday camp' arguments we see today in the press, it must be acknowledged that many women's lives were as impoverished outside the prison as they were inside, indeed they could have rougher lives and poorer diets than inside the prison system. Nevertheless, all of the women in prison shared a loss of liberty, loss of control over their lives and the domination of a prison regime.

In 1813, Elizabeth Fry described the women who were confined in Newgate Prison:

> 300 females of every category – tried, untried, felons, misdemeanants – with their numerous children. Many of these women were half naked, the rest in rags. They had no beds, and upon this floor whereupon they slept, they washed also, and cooked their food. On all sides the ear was assailed by awful imprecations, begging, swearing, singing, fighting, dancing, dressing up in men's clothes. The scenes are too bad to be described.

Fry's evidence to the House of Commons was reprinted in 1875 by Arthur Griffiths, ex-Governor of Millbank Prison. He wanted to draw a comparison between those unreformed prisons and the prison system of his day. Certainly, many things had changed over that sixty-year period. Many local prisons were renovated, or rebuilt, with better ventilation and heating, prison kitchens and limited medical facilities were established, and these gave local prisons a more ordered environment than Fry had experienced. In 1877 the prisons were brought under national jurisdiction, which gave them a more uniform governance structure and oversight.

Until the start of the twentieth century, all prisons had some accommodation for female prisoners (except for Wandsworth and Pentonville). There were unfulfilled plans to bring women together into a small number of female-only institutions, but this only happened in London when Westminster held all metropolitan female prisoners until it closed in 1883, and in Holloway after 1902. Across the country, in 1894 there was space for approximately 4,000 female prisoners in local prisons, which was less than a quarter of the prison estate. Capacity for local female prisoners stayed at about this level until the end of our period in the 1920s.

From the mid-nineteenth century onwards a small proportion of women experienced the convict system. After the mid-nineteenth century, only the most severe crimes were met with capital sentences, and the majority of public sentiment was against hanging women, increasingly conceptualised as weak, passive creatures in need of protection. As such the majority of even the most serious crimes were met with sentences of incarceration rather than death. Later in this book we describe two cases where women were not able to escape the gallows. Nevertheless, most women who were initially sentenced to death for their crimes had their sentence 'respited', and they were sentenced to life imprisonment in a convict prison. Although women made up around 20 per cent of the total prison population, just a few hundred at any one time were in the convict system.

Women sentenced to penal servitude in a convict prison were first held in a local prison until they were transferred to Millbank for nine months of solitary confinement, the better to ponder their moral weaknesses, until they were reassigned to a convict prison. For women, this meant being transported to Brixton (1853 to 1869) or Parkhurst (1864 to 1869). Some women were sent to Fulham Refuge or Woking Prison, as was the case with Mary Hardyman (see Chapter 20). The discipline in Fulham Refuge was less penal than in other convict prisons, and the women in their charge were trained in skills designed to gain them employment when they were released. This is not to say it was a soft touch – it was still very much part of the prison system, and in 1870 became a full convict prison for men and women. In the same year Parkhurst's and Brixton's doors were closed to women, and Woking opened as a purpose-built women's prison. When it closed in 1895 the women were transferred to Aylesbury in Buckinghamshire. As discussed in the case of Maria Adams (Chapter 18), convict prisons held only adults, while from the mid-century juveniles were diverted elsewhere.

The Reformatory and Industrial School system that was initially introduced to train and discipline wayward boys also contained girls (although, like convict prisons, they always made up a smaller proportion of children in the system). The reformatories reflected a wider attempt to deal with women and children outside of the formal disciplines of the local and convict prison system. Reformatories were part of a range of semi-penal institutions – homes, refuges, asylums and hospitals which women voluntarily attended or were ordered by the court to be confined in. Women were perceived as having weaker and more malleable minds than men, and were therefore, like young people, thought inherently more capable of reform than adult male offenders. This meant that they could be locked away in a variety of institutions, Ellen Coppin (see Chapter 29), for example, spent time in both an inebriates' home and a Lock Hospital rather than in a prison cell as a male offender might have done. This was a mixed blessing. Women could be 'saved' by spending years being reformed or refeminised (a key part of the process of reform), whilst a man sentenced for similar crimes would be out of a local prison in a matter of months. For women who had committed serious enough crimes to be sent to a convict prison, the perceived weakness of their minds caused them to be medicalised to a disproportionate degree. When women, such as Ann Griffiths (see Chapter 9), broke their cell furniture, sang in their cell at quiet time or used obscene language to warders, they were punished for their impulsive and emotional outbursts; and medical officers prescribed straitjackets and solitary confinement to cure their irrational behaviour. Dr Guy, the Medical Officer at Millbank, observed, 'If they are put in a dark cell, they shout and sing and make merry. They know that there are prisoners not very far off who can hear their noise, and they like to go on in that strange way.' In 1875, Arthur Griffiths, in *Memorials of Millbank* stated that:

> It is a well-established fact in prison logistics that the women are far worse than the men. When given to misconduct they are far more persistent in their evil ways, more outrageously violent, less amenable to reason or reproof … No doubt when a woman is really bad, when all the safeguards natural and artificial with which they have been protected are removed, further deterioration is sure to be rapid when it once begins.

While the Victorians saw such outbursts as further proof of women's instability, we as researchers and historians might perhaps interpret them as rather rational responses to the frustrations and constraints of the prison system. Where misbehaving women were perceived to be defiant, or incorrigible, rather than 'mad' they had their breaches of prison regulations punished with loss of remission (they had their early release pushed back), solitary confinement or with a reduced diet. This meant a penal diet of bread and water, although some prison governors hesitated to take food away from women. 'I do not think they can stand much dietary punishment ... some of them are not in the best of health' noted the Governor of Liverpool Prison; the Matron of Strangeways, Elizabeth Little, agreed that the penal diet 'lowered women too much'. Other punishments included the cropping of hair, wearing a heavy canvas jacket or being denied 'association' with other prisoners. There must also have been an array of informal and unofficial punishments meted out. Moreover, as Ann Griffith found out, resistance could result not only in being punished within the prison, but also the possibility of being removed to an institution for the mentally unstable, like Broadmoor Hospital.

If their minds were seen to be weak, women's bodies were still seen to be strong enough to carry out prison labour. Women who were sentenced to first-class hard labour were not put on the treadwheel, or sent to the quarries to break stone, and were not required to turn the crank, as men were. Instead they picked oakum. The unravelling of old Navy shipping rope was an arduous task, the tar-soaked hard and coarse strands of rope could cut fingers to pieces, and this miserable task must have been loathed by female prisoners. In comparison with the range of prison labour imposed on men, women had a smaller range of tasks they were made to complete. Happily for the authorities, they could exploit conceptions of natural female duties to help them lower the financial costs of imprisonment. The prison laundries and the prison kitchens were staffed with female convicts. Although both of those places provided companionship and warmth (in the winter this was welcome, though not in the summer), the work was hard. Women sentenced to second-class hard labour carried out sewing, knitting, mat-making, cleaning and sweeping. These 'feminine' tasks were useful to the running of the prison, as well as productively using the time of the female prisoners. When women were not working, they had time in their cells, mandatory religious services, were exercised in a prison yard or were able to freely associate with other prisoners in the hall. The friendships and alliances women made in those moments must have provided some comfort, and helped to fill the gap that absences of family created. The close relationships that women forged was perpetually problematic to the authorities – women fought with foes and enjoyed loving relationships with fellow prisoners (and with some warders). This was another way in which the secure estate found itself unable to adequately deal with female emotions.

After the first few years of the system had passed, no children were allowed in the convict prison. Women who were pregnant when they were sentenced had the children in a local prison and were then sent to a convict prison, or alternately were briefly transferred out of the convict prison to Westminster prison to give birth, and then back again. The child was not permitted to stay while the woman finished her sentence and instead was sent to family, the workhouse or sometimes to a religious or charitable institution. Women could communicate by letter with children and 'respectable' friends and family, although news from home could be distressing as Sarah Tuff found out (see Chapter 25). The authorities were keen to manage the relationships women had outside of the prison, and also those they made within the prison system. Informal relationships between female staff and prisoners were recognised as a realistic way of both controlling prisoners' behaviour and exerting moral influence. Not surprisingly, women who had been starved of affection in their lives would respond to kind words from a warder.

Clearly the mere existence and the daily control of female prisoners caused many problems for a penal policy which was orientated mainly towards male offenders. The operation of the prison and reformatory system reflected how the authorities dealt with those challenges, and therefore the experiences of female prisoners were different from those of men, even though housed in very similar institutions. For example, women journeyed through their sentences in progressive stages, just as men did, but with significant differences as they approached release. The following chapter explains how women progressed through their sentences until they were finally released.

Chapter 5

WOMEN AND POST-RELEASE SUPERVISION

As we discussed in the previous chapter, women progressed through their sentences just as men did, but with significant differences as they approached release. This chapter explains what happened to convict women as they progressed through the system, what stages they went through when they were approaching early release (being licensed, or earning their 'ticket-of-leave'), and how the authorities kept an eye on them once they regained their freedom.

Women who were gaoled in a local prison usually served the whole of their sentence in a single prison. Convict women experienced the prison 'churn', and often served their sentences in several prisons. This wasn't as haphazard as it seemed. The authorities hoped that the churn stopped harmful or difficult relationships forming between convict women – feuds, love-affairs or groups of difficult prisoners who could offer collective resistance to the system. There was also an order to the movement of prisoners. As previously explained, the first stage of penal servitude was spent in Millbank in solitary confinement, and then all prisoners were moved out to another convict prison. They then worked their way through progressive stages of their sentence. Each prisoner earned between six and eight marks per day based on the degree of effort they applied to the prison regime, and at each stage they would receive small benefits to alleviate their confinement. This might include being able to write or receive a letter, being permitted a visit from a relative, extra period of exercise during the week or being employed on easier tasks, e.g. feeding and looking after the prison farm animals. Each convict could also be credited with a small amount of money every day if they were of good behaviour in prison. This would be put in an account which would be given to the convict on the day of her release. Convicts progressed from probation class to third, second, first and then to special stage. Marks could be lost for breaches of the prison rules and regulations and prisoners could regress back to an earlier stage. The loss of marks reduced the number of days they had earned towards an early release, so the harder they worked, the better they behaved, the earlier they could expect to be released from their sentence. Because Maria Adams had racked up a number of prison offences, she was only released two months before she was due; others like Mary Hardyman served only half of the sentence imposed by the judge in court. Once they neared the end of their sentence, male and female convicts followed different routes. Men coming up to the formal expiration of their sentence in England and Wales were allowed to grow their hair out from the convict crew cut. Women only had their hair cropped as a punishment since the system desired them to look and act as close to contemporary ideals of femininity as possible. Women also served a period of time in a 'refuge' before release (although women who had already served a convict sentence and spent time in a refuge were unlikely to be granted a second opportunity).

Fulham Refuge was initially used as part of the staged rehabilitation process originally proposed by Lieutenant Colonel Jebb, Surveyor-General of Prisons and Chairman of the Directors of Convict Prisons. The refuge trained women in cooking, cleaning and laundry skills which could help the women to gain employment when they were released. Whilst Fulham Refuge was part of the convict system, there were other government- or privately funded refuges made available for female convicts: Carlisle Memorial Refuge at Winchester, Eagle House Refuge at Hammersmith for Roman Catholics and Westminster Memorial Refuge of the Royal Society for the Assistance of Discharged Prisoners for Protestant women. This last institution opened in 1872 and was based at 32 Charing Cross, Streatham, London. It was renamed as Russell House in 1888, when it became a refuge for reformed Roman Catholic prostitutes. East End House in Finchley, North London, was also funded and operated by the Catholic Church. During the 1870s and 1880s both refuges were used for women prisoners who entered their care for between six and nine months for a period on conditional licence before being fully licensed. After 1900 neither home received female convicts on conditional licence and instead they devoted their resources to supporting poor young women and girls. When women had completed their time in a refuge they received a conditional licence which allowed them to leave it and be 'at large' so long as they kept to certain regulations.

As will be seen in the lives of Elizabeth Dyer and Susannah Wells, women who were transported to Australia were released on a proto-probation scheme where they were assigned to employers after completing a period 'under sentence' working for the government. The scheme worked with varying degrees of success, but was much admired by Joshua Jebb. When transportation to the Australian penal colonies was coming to an end, Jebb decided to repatriate this part of the system. He was of the opinion that a system where freedom could be earned by good behaviour, and be taken away by re-offending, would be a better system than the pardoning scheme which had preceded it. Pardoning was indiscriminate, but licensing was able to discriminate down to the level of the single individual. It would help the authorities to watch over men and women and ensure that they had left the convict system as better people – at least that was Jebb's plan. He did, however, misjudge public opinion. The general public, who had known little of the workings of the convict system up to now, were not keen to have prisoners who had not served their full sentence wandering around the streets. Nevertheless, in England and Wales, approximately 1,300 prisoners a year were issued with licences between 1854 and 1919. This meant that approximately a quarter of the sentenced prison population was released on licence each year. The system continued, was gradually extended in scope to take in local prisoners and is still in effect today.

When released, each convict was given a Bible and Prayer Book and was accompanied to the nearest railway station by a prison officer, who then gave them a railway ticket to their stated destination. Licence-holders remained free so long as they met certain conditions.

They would lose the licence if they committed another offence; they were also expressly forbidden from associating with 'notoriously bad characters', leading 'an idle or dissolute life' or having 'no visible means of support'. If anyone lost their licence, they were returned to prison to serve the residue of their sentence. Between 1864 and 1869 all male convicts on licence also had to report on a weekly basis to a police station in their residential district, after that it was monthly. The system had men in mind, but applied equally to women, with some exceptions. Female licence-holders reported only once to the police force, and once to the female superintendent of the refuge where they were registered. They were then under no further obligation to report, but female superintendents were encouraged to keep an eye on all women after they had left the refuge. For both men and women, the reporting system was, at best, variable, and was largely abandoned by the 1880s.

There was one further form of support available to men and women after they walked through the prison gates. By 1884 every prison, with the exception of Oxford, had established a discharged prisoners' aid society. They would provide a few days' accommodation for those who did not have a home to go to, and could provide reading glasses, boots, and other kinds of practical aid. The Chaplain of Worcester prison recorded that financial assistance they provided had allowed four women to go to a home at Wakefield, and he had received word back that they were 'conducting themselves satisfactorily and desire to express their gratitude for the opportunity afforded them of regaining their characters and obtaining honest employment'. The main aim of the DPAS was to provide a bridge between prison and employment, and between the 1890s and 1920s they managed to build relationships with sympathetic employers who would take in reformed ex-convicts.

A letter sent to the editor of *The Spectator* on 24 February 1923 both advertised the services of the DPAS and revealed the difficulties experienced by recently released prisoners:

It is impossible to imagine a more forlorn position than that of a discharged prisoner when he steps from the prison gate to face life afresh, dogged and haunted by the past. For many the worst sentence is not that pronounced by the judge, which has, at least, its limitation, but the life-long sentence of social ostracism pronounced by society. The plight of a woman or girl is even more tragic and fraught with graver possibilities to society and herself. She is often friendless, always without character, and in some cases with a child to support. These poor creatures have been known to tramp about London for weeks, heart-sick and weary, afraid to pawn their clothes for food lest a destitute appearance should take away their last chance of work, until courage fails and they either give false testimonials or commit thefts which bring them back to prison or practise the ghastly trade which is always open to such wanderers. The Holloway Discharged Prisoners' Aid Society, which is the only Discharged Prisoners' Aid Society dealing with discharged women and girls, has been in existence eighteen years, and during that time has assisted thousands of women.

Given that having a criminal past was a considerable burden to gaining employment and establishing a new life outside of prison, some ex-convicts simply changed names and left town to start again under an assumed identity. They therefore breached the conditions of their licence, but that wasn't a problem unless they got caught. That, of course, was considerably problematic to the authorities. It was considered especially important to continue surveillance beyond the prison gate, and beyond the licence period, for habitual offenders who were likely to commit further offences.

Accordingly, the 1869 Habitual Offender Act was brought in to mandate minimum prison sentences for those who had committed two indictable offences, but also at least three years supervision by the police. As well as increased reporting stipulations (fortnightly to the local police station) this gave the police the power to stop anyone on the Habitual Offender Register. Anyone who could not prove they were making an honest living could be sent to custody for twelve months. Similarly, anyone on the register who was living with, or drinking with, known thieves or prostitutes could be imprisoned. In effect, it extended the conditional licences years into the future for a number of ex-convicts – in fact, a very large number. Because the police could not cope with the huge number of ex-convicts they now had to supervise (25,000 in the first two years of the 1869 Act), the 1871 Prevention of Crimes Act gave the judiciary the discretion to impose police supervision or not. In the cases of Maria Allen, they did. The 1871 Act mandated that up to seven years post-release from prison, any convict found guilty of living by dishonest means, caught giving false details to a court, found on enclosed premises with the intent to commit a felony or even just acting suspiciously in an enclosed area, could be sent to prison for twelve months.

Supervision is not necessarily a bad thing. Probation today also imposes a level of supervision and surveillance and is designed to be supportive. Having the police made responsible for carrying out the supervision, however, was clearly not the best way of going about this – many officers took it upon themselves to tell employers that their new worker was 'an ex-con' for example – and the system talked of grinding people into good citizens, which was a depressing and ineffective approach. Current research shows that the Habitual Offender Acts were hard to operate and counter-productive, and that both female and male ex-convicts continued to experience considerable challenges in finding a new life for themselves after they left prison behind.

Part 2

CASE STUDIES OF CRIMINAL WOMEN

Chapter 6

AMELIA SACH

(B. 1867 HAMPRESTON, DORSET) – EXECUTED

Born in Dorset on 5 May 1867 to parents Francis and Georgina, Frances Amelia Thorne married a builder called Jeffrey Sach in 1896. Her father, who had been a bricklayer and a fruit-dealer, was by then a gardener living in Lewisham, London. At the time of the marriage Amelia was managing a 'lying-in' home in Stanley Road which assisted women to give birth, and provided a room for the new mother to receive guests and visitors. Later she opened up a similar service at Claymore House in Hertford Road (both properties were in Finchley, London).

Around 1900, she advertised, 'Doctor recommends comfortable home, skilled nurses, every care, comfortable home – Nurse, 4, Stanley-road, East Finchley.' There was a charge for assisting birth, and another fee for arranging an adoption in the form of a 'present' of around £30 to the future parents of the child. Most of the women who used their services were domestic servants, sometimes women who had been impregnated by their employers or by men to whom they were not married. This would have been a very profitable business, even had it been operating as advertised. In Sach's case, the business was a front for a much more sinister trade which came to light in 1903. The *Echo* reported on 16 January that Sach and a co-defendant Walters were charged with the wilful murder of an unnamed infant. The trial took place at the Old Bailey.

Several witnesses, unnamed in press reports, and one witness who was allowed to give evidence without ever being identified to the court, stated that they had contracted to have babies adopted at Claymore House. The prosecution produced medical evidence from

Dr Joseph Pepper, the Divisional Police Surgeon who had carried out the post-mortem examination of the body of the child found dead. He testified that the child had died from suffocation caused by a narcotic poison. The prosecutor pressed him,

> Would the death be consistent with the administration of chlorodyne? 'It would'. The Judge then intervened so say that, 'A witness has stated that she heard the child making a peculiar noise … can you account for the child making those noises?'. Dr Pepper replied, 'I was in Court and heard the witness imitate the noise … I should say they were dying gasps.'

The co-defendant in the case, Mrs Walters, attempted to distance herself from this damning evidence. She insisted that 'Sach had told her that she received no money for the babies. In her opinion 'the mothers were heartless things, leaving them on her hands. I was greatly surprised to hear she received so much money from the mothers, and you know the rest.' Walters was reported as sitting stolidly in court, not a muscle of her face moving. However, neither of their defences were helped by the medical evidence nor by the fact that a large quantity of baby clothes found at Claymore House indicated the scale of their crimes.

Unlike Walters, Sach seemed 'terribly curious not to miss a word of what was said, and when, in the case of several of the witnesses, the answers given to questions of counsel were, but faintly uttered, and difficult to hear, she placed her head on one side, and wrinkled her brow as though greatly annoyed at having missed a word'. The *Echo* continued that

> the Court was tense and the atmosphere close. Not only were the three little boxes which serve as accommodation for the public between the squat pillars overlooking the dock packed to excess, with the front rows filled with females, but every available seat in the well of the Court was occupied, and counsel, in wig and gown, and others carrying top-hats were crowded together, standing on the staircase leading to the lobby of the Courts. (*Echo*, 16 January 1903)

Unattributed illustration, printed in the 1903 Echo, of Sach and her co-defendant in the dock.

Murder trials always attracted an audience, of course, but this case had attracted more attention than most. In the final address, Mr Leycester, Sach's defence advocate, stated that the prosecution had not proved their case. He argued that it had not even been proved that there had been a murder. The babies, when they left the custody of Mrs Sach, were alive and well, he insisted. The jury disagreed, and brought in a verdict of 'guilty'. The judge announced that the death sentence would be imposed on both women.

A local campaign to have their sentences commuted to life was unsuccessful, and Amelia Sach became the first woman to be hanged in London's new women's prison at Holloway on 3 February 1903 (previously hangings had taken place at Newgate Prison). Both Sachs and Walters were buried in unmarked graves within the walls of Holloway Prison, as was customary. The bodies were exhumed in 1971 when Holloway underwent renovation, and the bodies were reburied in Brookwood Cemetery. This time their names were inscribed on a grey granite tombstone. The nameplate of Claymore House, on the other hand, was chiselled off after the trial, and has never been reinstated.

Chapter 7

VIOLET WATSON

(B. 1896 GLASGOW) – REFORMATORY GIRL

Not all children who ended up in reformatory schools were 'pint-sized pickpockets' from 'broken homes', or violent unmanageable girls. Yet one thing all inmates had in common was the challenge they posed to authority, something that did not necessarily end once they were locked away behind reformatory walls.

Violet Watson was born in Glasgow in 1896. Her father William was a photographer, who would tour the country setting up temporary studios, or practising street photography to make a living. Violet's mother, Mary, followed him and looked after Violet and her three sisters (and later two younger brothers).

Violet was a precocious child, who found the regime of her school too punitive for her liking. In 1909, at the age of 15, Violet left Glasgow for Perth, without notifying her parents where she was going, and upon arrival began canvassing for donations to what she called the 'School Revelation Fund'. She claimed she was doing so on behalf of her father, who once the sum of £50 had been raised, intended to challenge the Glasgow School Board about the harsh punishments they imposed on pupils. In Perth, a fellow traveller purchased Violet a ticket for Aberdeen, to which she duly travelled and set up in the Bon-Accord Hotel asking visitors for donations. Violet was quickly apprehended and brought to the police court where she was tried with impersonating an insurance agent, with the intention to defraud the public. It transpired that, not only did Violet's father have no knowledge of her plan, he did not even have the money required to bring her back home to Glasgow. Instead, Violet was sentenced

Sunderland Reformatory.

to spend three years in the Loanhead Reformatory for Girls in Edinburgh.

If Violet had found the regime at her school too harsh, it is no surprise that she found life in the reformatory even harder and less palatable. She fermented revolt. As one of the older girls at the reformatory, Violet wasted no time in rallying fellow pupils to join her cause. Less than a year after her arrival, in November 1910, *The Scotsman* reported that the girls were in 'OPEN REBELLION':

> Unruly conduct on the part of the girls under sentence of detention in the Dalry Reformatory Loanhead, has led to some extraordinary scenes recently. It appears that the girls have got almost totally out of hand and the girls have been escaping from the institution since September. The girls' ages range from twelve to seventeen years and many are employed at laundry work. There are about 40 inmates in the Reformatory at present ... The trouble first manifested itself in class-rooms where several of the elder and bigger

girls threatened to black the teacher's eyes and danced jingo-rings. Later some of the girls mounted the roof of the building and escaped by means of the drain pipe. Last week Mid-Lothian police were engaged until midnight looking for six girls who had escaped. On Monday the girls broke out in open revolt and a number escaped, considerable difficulty being experienced in bringing them back.

Violet, was one of the main ringleaders, and had managed to make her own daring escape. Captured towards the end of November, Violet was brought to the Edinburgh Police court with her two conspirators Rosanna Murdoch and Jean Miller. The trio were accused not only of their own unlawful escapes, but of being responsible for the breakdown of order at the reformatory, and of facilitating the escape of sixteen other girls. The sheriff intended to make an example of the girls, sentencing Miller and Murdoch to three weeks in prison, and sending Violet, not yet 16, back to the reformatory she hated.

Less than two weeks later, Violet was back at the Edinburgh sheriff's court, having escaped again from the reformatory. Violet had somehow managed to procure money from inside the reformatory, and had made her way to the railway station, travelling to Govan, and then back to Glasgow. She was captured four days later and taken back to Edinburgh. The sheriff vowed that everything that had occurred at the Dalry Reformatory would be 'wiped out' and that Violet, as ringleader of the insurrection, would not be allowed to return. She was sent instead to a reformatory in Sunderland, to be detained there at the pleasure of the Secretary for Scotland. Violet was told that if she behaved in Sunderland, she would not experience further punishment, and that if her good behaviour continued, she might actually be released in just a few weeks.

Three months later, Violet was still in the Sunderland reformatory. Finding it no more enjoyable to be in than the Dalry Reformatory and with the promise of quick release coming to nothing, Violet made another daring escape. Climbing out of an attic window and onto the roof of the reformatory, Violet made her way down to the ground, and then scaled the perimeter wall, which had shards of broken glass fixed along its length. Violet made it over to the other side, but badly cut her arm in the process, leaving a trail of blood behind her. She made her way through Sunderland, begging strangers for help, and was eventually taken into a house to have her wound dressed. A local policeman had no trouble tracing Violet's path, and she was apprehended just hours after her escape. Now 16, Violet could be held to the full account of the law. She was sentenced to two months' imprisonment, which she served at Durham prison.

Prison was a harder environment than reformatory school. Facing severe punishment for disobedience, and unable to escape, Violet had no choice but to serve her time. She was released in June 1911 and, finally free of the institutions she hated, returned to Scotland. At the age of 16, she was not required to return to school, and so was free to build a respectable life for herself.

Violet was not typical of most girls who ended up in reformatory schools. She came from a respectable working-class family, she did not steal through poverty or want, was not violent or conventionally unruly. Her two years in the penal system occurred primarily because of her objection to the poor treatment of children by the institutions designed to cater for them. After her release, Violet married and settled in London. She was never convicted again, and as far as records allow us to know, she went on to have a perfectly ordinary life with no hint of the teenage renegade inside her re-emerging.

Chapter 8

ANN GRIFFITH

(B. 1845 BRADFORD, YORKS) – BROADMOOR NO. 331

Ann was born in Bradford, but spent a lot of her time defending herself in the courts of York. A married factory-hand with three children, she was convicted many times of drunkenness, theft and disorder (over fifty times in fact). Once again serving a short prison sentence in Her Majesty's Prison York Castle, Ann made an error which would condemn her to many years of confinement. In an act of defiance, she set fire to the curtain which covered her cell window. Charged with the serious crime of arson she was tried at York Assizes on 14 July 1877 and sentenced to fifteen years' penal servitude in a convict prison.

Along with other convicts, she was sent first to Millbank Prison in London before being assigned a prison where she would serve the bulk of her sentence. The Millbank Penal Record stated she was

> A woman of violent temper and a more than average physical strength. Is unwilling to submit to authority and has recourse to violence with a view to gaining her own ends. Has shown on several occasions here that she is able to exercise self-control when she has sufficient motive for doing so. Often says she is sometimes inclined to take her own life rather than go through the long period of penal servitude to which she has been sentenced.

This view was echoed by the Medical Officer at Woking Prison, her next port of call. He noted that Ann had a

Surrey County Asylum at Tooting.

Violent and unrestrained temper, sometimes seems quite crazy. Fights with her fellow prisoners whenever she has the opportunity. General health fairly good. Scrofulous contusions [scrofula was a swelling caused by tuberculosis] on the right side of neck. Has pain in heart. A woman of large frame and muscular development. Does not sleep well. Wants nourishment – promises to behave well.

Over the next few years Ann broke many prison rules and regulations – smashing her cell furniture, destroying her clothes, shouting, insolence, swearing and so on – and received heavy punishment in return. She was stripped naked, her head shaved, was incapacitated with chloroform, and restrained in a straitjacket on many occasions often for long periods of time. In February 1880, there was 'a sign, but not a very hopeful one, that she finds the strait jacket unyielding. She now asks for release'. By May, following

51

more distress from Ann, and brutal prison disciplinary punishments being applied, the Prison Medical Officer stated that 'This woman is (whether sane or insane) most assuredly a demonised termagant and requires firm and continuous repression.' He requested that Ann be removed to Broadmoor Hospital in Berkshire, which she was, on 4 February 1881.

The Broadmoor patient file revealed some interesting and hidden parts of Ann's history. The record stated she had previously been admitted to Broadmoor before (for eight months) whilst she was serving another prison sentence. This again came about because she resisted the prison authorities. In attempting to diagnose her current mental condition, the Broadmoor doctors could find no reasonable explanation. However, they noted that:

> she says that in 1871 she had wool put in her head after severe injury. Good bodily health. Dangerous to others. Probably congenital. Of intemperate habits herself. Intemperate father, mother, uncle. Chief delusions around food, and her general treatment. A woman who has led a very intemperate and turbulent life; is a dangerous ill-conditioned convict with little power of self-control. Has strange notions, possibly delusions, regarding her food. No epilepsy. Very intemperate, when free.

This was the usual jumble of potential causes, chief of which was usually a congenital weakness passed down the family-line, or mental instability caused by too much alcohol.

The Broadmoor authorities obviously thought there was an underlying psychosis which came to the fore when she was either drunk or when subjected to the extreme pressures put upon many people by the experience of serving a long-term prison sentence. The environment at Broadmoor was designed to be secure, but therapeutic, with the aim of bringing about mental stability and re-entry to society, rather than punishment, and the environment was much more appropriate for women like Ann Griffiths. Her time at Broadmoor appears to be less disruptive, whether that was because she liked the food better, had no access to alcohol, had better treatment from the authorities than she had in Millbank and Woking Prisons or for some other reason. We will never know because the records do not describe her treatment whilst in the hospital.

We also do not know what happened to Ann after she was discharged. She was due to leave Broadmoor in 1892, but there is no trace of her in the 1901 census (when she would have been 56). She may have gone back to York to be with her husband or her by-now grown-up children; she may have decided to stay in the Berkshire area, or perhaps she died before the census was taken. The only thing we do know, however, is that she was never re-admitted to Broadmoor.

Chapter 9

ANN NICHOLLS

(B. 1842 LINTHORPE, YORKS) – BROADMOOR NO. 188

In 1865 Ann Richmond began her married life with Richard Nicholls in Stockton-on-Tees, in north-east England. Richard had found work as a puddler in an iron works, which was the main form of employment in Middlesbrough; and by 1871 Ann and Richard had three children. The oldest, aged 4, was named after his father; Mary was aged 2, and James was aged just four months. Two months later, however, James's life was cut short, and his mother stood in the dock accused of his murder. One afternoon, she had administered vitriol to the baby, which had caused very severe burning to the child's hands, face and neck. Death would have been very painful, and the sight which greeted the witnesses as they rushed into help would have been pitiful.

Ann was charged with wilful murder, tried at Durham Assizes, and found not guilty due to insanity. The judge ordered Ann to be detained at Her Majesty's Pleasure. This meant that she would be kept in a secure environment and could (at least in theory) be brought back to court at any time to serve a prison sentence. This was a legal device, where those who were unfit to plead, or who were clearly mentally unbalanced at the time of the crime, could receive treatment well away from the public gaze.

Ann was admitted to Broadmoor Hospital for Criminal Lunatics on 25 July 1871, aged 30. The files show that, although the courts had found her to be insane at the time of the murder, she now appeared to be quite sane: 'Has been free from any symptom since admission. Good health. Not suicidal. Cause of insanity unknown. Delusions: none whilst in prison. No sign of epilepsy, not known if temperate or intemperate, Roman Catholic, imperfect education.'

issey. On going into the house, witness saw Mrs Nicholls sitting on the bedside in her bedroom. Mrs Nicholls was crying. Witness asked her what was the matter with her. Prisoner replied, " Nothing is the matter with me, but I have killed the baby." Witness asked prisoner where the baby was, and the reply was " In the back room." Witness then went into the back room, and there saw the baby lying in the bed quite dead. The baby was undressed, but with a nightgown flung over the body. The child's mouth, neck, and hands were black. A hole was burnt in the pillow on which the child was lying. On witness returning to the room where Mrs Nicholls was sitting, she asked her if the poison in the bottle had been given to the baby by mistake. Mrs Nicholls replied, " I gave the right bottle ; but do not know what made me do it." Prisoner was crying very much, and said she wished she could bring the baby back again. Did not hear prisoner say anything about the other children. Had previously heard prisoner complain of being low-spirited. Prisoner had always appeared fond of her children. The

Middlesbrough Daily Gazette, *13 Dec. 1871.*

Her sanity was also never questioned by her husband, who wrote to Broadmoor in 1873 to ask if his wife could be discharged. The couple intended to leave the country for Germany to start a new life. Dr Orange, the Broadmoor Superintendent, replied that it would do no harm to apply, but he was generally pessimistic about their chances. He was right. Two years later, Broadmoor were still reporting that'there is no change in either her state of health, or in her general conduct. She may still be considered as sane. With the exemption of headaches from which she suffers occasionally her bodily health is good, but the recurrence from time to time of headaches indicates that the patient might not improbably relapse if subjected to anxiety or trouble'.

In 1877 some of Ann's friends asked if it was possible to petition again for her release, and the following year, her husband petitioned once more for her early release. Broadmoor responded.

> Ann Nicholls has not, to my knowledge, shown any sign of mental aberration or depression during that time in an equitable and even cheerful frame of mind, and at work in the laundry. She is sane and appears to have been so for several years, and I believe that, under ordinary circumstances, she might without insurmountable risk, be discharged to the care of her husband who is prepared and anxious for her to share the comforts of his home in America (Pittsburg). No doubt, if she again became pregnant and had children (being 38 years of age) there would be risk of relapse (more or less temporary) into insanity so that at such periods, special care and attention would have to be exercised.

This time the appeal was successful and she was discharged in the spring of 1878. She then sailed across the Atlantic on the steamship *Greece* to join her husband in New York.

Shortly after they were reunited, her husband sent a letter back to Broadmoor thanking them for their kindness and care. The family home was now 33 Penn St, in Pittsburgh.

> Rest assured that I shall faithfully observe and carry out the conditions upon which she was released for my own comfort and duty will ever prompt me that way. She is now in the best of health and it will be my greatest earthly aim to keep her so. The faithfulness with which I have held to my wife during so long and trying a period will be I hope a sufficient proof to you to give you sincerity of my intentions. With a sincere prayer for the welfare of yourself and yours.

The 1880 US Federal Census showed that she was still living in Pittsburgh with husband and children, and with their newly born son, Ferdinand. They seem then to have moved to Ohio sometime after 1885. The Nicholls joined many other families who were moving westwards during this time, as new economic opportunities opened up. Ann appears to have died sometime between 1900 and 1910 (she appears in the 1900 US Federal Census but not the 1910 Census), and her widowed husband who had stood by her all those years continued to work as a night-watchman, living in rented accommodation with his daughter and grandchildren, until he died.

So, despite committing one of the most serious crimes, and suffering from post-natal depression, and also, let us not forget, coping with living in a secure institution for a number of years, Ann was able to remake her life in a new country. With the support of Broadmoor, and of her very supportive husband, she was able to have more children, and enjoy family life in Pittsburgh and Ohio long after she had walked through Broadmoor's gates.

Chapter 10

ELEANOR BONIFACE ALIAS ELLEN KNIGHT

(B. 1837 LONDON) – CONVICT 10/1/609

Eleanor Jones was born in London in the same year that Queen Victoria took to the throne. She was convicted of numerous offences in her twenties, but first found trouble when only a teenager. Eleanor served two custodial sentences in 1852 (six months) and 1853 (eighteen months) at the age of 15 and 16 respectively. Then, in 1856 she appeared at the Old Bailey under the assumed name of Ellen Knight. The charge this time was counterfeiting coins, a serious offence which could attract a long prison sentence, and had it been just five years earlier might have seen her transported to Australia. The court heard that retired Police Inspector James Brannan had forced his way into a house in Russell Square looking for a counterfeiting gang. He found Eleanor (or Ellen) and her co-defendant Isaac Knight, crouching over a hot fire. Brannan seized a plaster-of-Paris mould, and some recently minted counterfeit coins, and then apprehended the two prisoners. Ellen complained that she had been assaulted during the raid: 'When the man was holding me down on the bed with the hair of my head, did you not strike me with your clenched fist?' 'No, never – it was as much as two of us could do to hold you on the bed, you were so violent.' Although she stated that she was unmarried, Isaac alleged that Eleanor (or Ellen) was his lawful wife, and should be treated with respect, 'This woman is my lawful wife, I can assure you; we were married at St. Pancras New Church'. Ellen then changed her mind and stated that she was actually married to Isaac, and that she could produce a marriage certificate. Both parties then pleaded guilty and were each sentenced to four years' penal servitude. This was not the last time they would find themselves in court, nor face to face with James Brannan.

When Ellen and Isaac (now under the names of Eleanor and Isaac Boniface) appeared at the Old Bailey in 1864, four years after the expiry of their former sentence, James Brannan, now an inspector working for the Royal Mint, was their accuser once again. Brannan had raided a counterfeiter's factory, and the circumstances he discovered were almost identical. Eleanor and Isaac were stooped over a bright light, filling plaster moulds with molten metal (melted down spoons). Brannan took a bucket of water and threw it on the fire, which put it out, and found three counterfeit sixpences, quite hot and unfinished. Again, in his evidence he stated that, when arrested, 'the female prisoner was exceedingly violent'.

The court again concerned itself with the couple's marital status. Brannan was brought back into court to testify that he 'was present at the trial of Isaac Knight and Eleanor Knight in 1856; the prisoners are the same persons – to the best of my recollection the woman stated then that she was married to the man in the name of Knight'. Eleanor Boniface produced her marriage certificate dated 12 November 1864, on which the name of Robert Charlton appeared as a witness, and the case was postponed for an hour at the prisoner's request (Charlton could not be found, but his wife said she couldn't remember Eleanor or Isaac at all). Isaac then chipped in to say that he had been 'in Liverpool in 1856 – I married my wife on 12th November, 1860 – I was living in East-street, and had lived there four months before – I left, I think, in 1857 – I lived there thirteen months with my present wife.' In fact, despite Isaac's shaky memory of events, the Lambeth Parish Registers prove that an Eleanor Jones had married Isaac Boniface in 1860, the year their sentence for the 1856 coining offence expired. Despite the fascination of the rest of the court, the Old Bailey judges were probably less interested in the nuptials than with proving that Eleanor and Isaac were repeat offenders who had already served lengthy prison sentences. Both defendants were sentenced to ten years' penal servitude each.

*Counterfeit note from the 'Bank of Engraving' (http://www.guywoolnough.com/
tag/bank-of-engraving/).*

In August 1870, having served more than half of her sentence,
Eleanor was granted early release. She was first released on a
conditional licence to the Battery House Refuge in Winchester, and
on 11 March 1871 she was licensed to Fulham Refuge, before finally
being released. Returning to Lambeth, she was never reunited with
Isaac. In 1871, whilst still serving his sentence, Isaac was confined in
Woking Invalid Prison because of his ailing health. He died in 1872
aged 48. The couple had spent more than half of their twelve-year
marriage confined in separate prisons. In 1881 the census reveals
that Eleanor was living as a widowed laundress in Lambeth. She was
not living on her own though. Also in the house were her two sons,
George, aged 8, and Robert aged 3. It seems that Eleanor had found a
new romantic partner to replace Isaac; and although she never lived

with her new partner (or partners, as the two boys may have had different fathers) she lived with her sons for a number of years. She was still living in Lambeth with George in 1891, when she herself was working as a sick-nurse. She died in Lambeth aged 62.

During her lifetime, Eleanor had a number of names and a number of relationships. Some documented, others not. The most meaningful were the romantic and working relationship she had with Isaac; and, ironically, the unwelcome relationship she had with James Brannan. Had it not been the same detective who arrested her in 1856 and in 1864 she might have persuaded the judge that this was her first offence (that was, after all, what the adoption of aliases was supposed to achieve) but with the same accuser in court that was impossible. All hope of a light sentence evaporated, and Isaac and Eleanor were sent to different convict prisons, never to see each other again.

Chapter 11

MARY ANN GANNON

(B. 1857 MANCHESTER) – LOCAL PRISONER

Mary Ann Gannon was born in Manchester in 1857 to Ellen and John Gannon, two Irish migrants who had settled in the Ancoats district of the city. As a child Mary suffered from smallpox, which left her permanently scarred, and she developed a speech impediment. Mary Ann's mother and older sister, Bridget, worked in one of Manchester's cotton factories, a trade Mary herself entered at the age of just 14.

Factory work brought young women like Mary into contact with a new social circle of workers of all ages, and saw them earn money of their own for the first time, although wages for a hard week's labour were often subsumed into the household budget with the worker given just a few shillings of 'pocket money' from their own wage packet. This was almost certainly the case for Mary, whose own earnings would have been needed by her mother to keep the family out of dire poverty after the death of Mary's father in the mid-1860s.

Young and inexperienced factory workers could soon find themselves in trouble, led astray by older women, or exhilarated by their new sense of freedom. Female factory workers in Manchester were often portrayed in the press as overly keen on drink and disorderly in their conduct. The newspapers disapproved of 'gangs' of factory women leaving work and going down the streets singing, towards the public houses. It was not public drunkenness that was Mary's problem, however.

Mary's first brush with the law came when she was just 15, in 1871, when she was sentenced to spend one month carrying out hard labour in a local prison. Mary and a friend had stolen a pair of boots

Machinery in a cotton mill.

from a local shop. The following year, after losing one of her fingers in an accident at the factory, Mary was again convicted of larceny and sentenced to another month of hard labour. It was around this time that Mary stopped living with her family, and began lodging with friends around Manchester instead.

Mary's hand and arm may have become infected after her initial injury, or another accident at the factory may have been to blame, but just months later, Mary's entire left arm had been amputated. Her employers would have accepted no liability for Mary's accident, and she would have been entitled to no compensation for the loss of her arm. Work would now be harder to find, and with only one arm, Mary would probably only have been eligible for the lowest paying roles.

At the age of 17, in 1875, Mary was convicted of breaking and entering and stealing items from the house of Agnes Pope, and she spent six months in prison. Upon release, she was found to be drunk and riotous in the street, and given another fourteen days. Because of the prison sentences, Mary lost her job. She began working on Manchester's streets as a prostitute, and it wasn't long until she was prosecuted for plying her new trade. Prostitution was a dangerous and low-paying job, and like many prostitutes in this period, Mary took the opportunity to occasionally relieve her customers of some of their more valuable belongings. In 1877, and again in 1878, Mary was convicted of robbery from the person.

Mary began using a range of different names in an attempt to avoid detection. She alternated between using her real surname and the assumed name 'Brandon', and occasionally went by her mother's name, Ellen Sheldon. However, her physical description made her easily identifiable and her aliases did little to curb her growing criminal record. With a number of convictions already against her, and many for serious property crimes, Mary was a clear candidate for a term of penal servitude. However, while she continued to serve significant periods of time in local prisons – one or two months for a theft, and on one occasion nine months for being an 'incorrigible rogue' – and having accumulated more than twenty-five convictions by 1880, she was never actually sentenced to spend time in a convict prison.

Mary's criminal record continued to grow during the early 1880s, however, and she was identified as a 'habitual criminal'. Yet the same thing that may have contributed to Mary's transition from a petty juvenile offender to an adult offender, and perhaps the factor that contributed most to her continued need to offend – the loss of her arm – may have been what saved her time and again from admission to convict prison. While local prisons were used to processing hundreds of criminals a year and incarcerating a diverse cross-section of the population for short periods, the convict system was not equipped to deal with prisoners with different needs. A serious impairment like the loss of a limb would have posed both the inmate and the institution a problem when it came to adhering to the strict routine of work, domestic duties and movement around the prison. Perhaps for this reason, Mary was left to her cycle of offending, short imprisonments and reoffending for more than a decade.

Something in Mary's life changed in 1886 when she attempted to drown herself in a Manchester canal. Whilst the man who rescued Mary was given an award by the Humane Society, Mary was put on trial for the crime of attempted suicide. Her defence stated that she had not attempted suicide, but fallen in on account of drunkenness, and been so intoxicated that she did not remember anything about the event. The truth of the matter was something that only Mary would ever know, but the jury acquitted her and she was discharged.

Mary's offending ceased for a number of years in the 1890s, and she relied heavily on the workhouse before she disappeared from all official records. She may have resumed offending and used a different alias, of course, although with only one arm and a distinctive speech impediment she would have remained easily identifiable to local constables and courts. No record of marriage exists for her, but she may have taken the name of someone with whom she had a significant relationship or cohabited. She may have moved on from Manchester, to start life afresh elsewhere, although problems finding well-paying work, and a stable life, would have remained. It is most likely, however, with few friends and estranged from her family, that Mary may simply have died, leaving little official record of her last years in poverty and obscurity.

Chapter 12

ELIZA CONNER AND MARY LEONARD

(B. 1827 AND 1826) – TRANSPORTED

The Old Bailey courtroom was full of accusations and a spirited defence in 1850. Two females in their early twenties were in the dock accused of robbery in a public park. The victim, John Bass, was the first to give his evidence:

> On 3rd May I was in Clapham Park – the prisoners followed me a considerable distance – there were gas-lamps, and I could see their faces – Leonard came up to me on the right side, caught me by the arm with her left-hand, and asked me how I did, and to go home with her – I said, 'No, I don't want you' – I just put her away – she laid hold of me by the collar with her left-hand – I slightly turned my head to disengage myself, and perceived a man – Leonard applied a heavy blow to my mouth, which I thought was with a handkerchief, or some soft substance, but it stunned me – before I could recover myself, I was struck a heavy blow with a fist on the back of my head which stunned me – it was from neither of the women – I fell on my left side – Leonard threw herself on the top of me, and at the same moment I received several severe kicks in the back, which could not be from a woman – Leonard kept the handkerchief to my mouth – I resisted all I could to keep it away, for I suspected there was something deleterious which I was to inhale – I smelt something unpleasant, but the time was so short

I could inhale but a very little – Conner laid hold of my watch – she had a difficulty to get it out, but she did … Leonard got her hand into my pocket with the money, and took some out … I lost half-a-sovereign and about 8s. – I called 'Police!' and 'Murder!' and a policeman came.

The police officer corroborated much of this evidence:

I heard cries of 'Murder!' and 'Police!' and found Bass on the ground … he seemed quite stupified from alarm and confusion – I have known him fourteen years, and never knew him tipsy – he is a very respectable man – he kept calling 'Police!' I stood him up on his legs, and took the prisoners in charge – when we had got about fifty yards towards the station, Leonard said to Conner, who was about ten yards behind, 'I would have stopped the old b—r's hallooing if I had known I should be caught like this, the b—y old thief; I would.'

One of the accused women, Eliza Conner, then interrupted the officer's testimony, 'Was not he in such a state of intoxication that he required two policemen?' 'The police constable replied that the victim was injured and had needed the two constables to help him home. The accused Mary Leonard then countered 'You said you would let us go, and take him to the station … When we went up we found him lying there on his back'. Given the strength of evidence against them, and the fact that they both had previous convictions for robbery, they were unsurprisingly found guilty and sentenced to be transported to Australia for fifteen years.

Both were transported on the *Emma Eugenia* convict ship, which deposited them in Hobart Town in Van Diemen's Land on 7 March 1851. What happened to the two women in their new homes? Did they continue in their offending ways, or did the salutary experience of the long voyage, spending time in custody in Hobart and the repeated work assignments convince them to change their ways?

The convict ship Emma Eugenia.

It seems that Eliza Conner did not take easily to her work assignments. She was apprehended by a constable for absconding from her employer whilst in company with a sailor in a singing room in Liverpool Street, and was sentenced to twelve months' imprisonment with hard labour. She was then reconvicted of absconding from the service of Mr Arthur Smith of Ross, on 21 December 1856. The local newspaper said that she received twelve months' hard labour because it was her third offence, but in fact this penalty was fairly standard. The reason for absconding may have been that Eliza wanted to spend more time with her new husband. Eliza was unmarried when she was transported (although she was living with Edward Conner and had taken his name). She married Thomas Rooney in Ross in 1855, but it would be almost four years before she earned her conditional release on 3 May 1859, allowing them to live together properly as man and wife. Things looked up for Eliza when she received a conditional pardon in 1862, granting her much more freedom to live and work in the colony. Eliza enjoyed her liberty for four years before she found herself back in court. In 1866 she was charged with assaulting her neighbour. She was lucky that the magistrates' bench imposed only a small fine.

Eliza was still not completely free of convict regulations at this time, and she was charged with not having informed the authorities that she had moved house. She had actually moved into her employer's house and Eliza pleaded guilty. Her employer was in court to speak up for her. Mr Pearce stated that Eliza had been in his service five months and 'a better servant he never had'. The case was dismissed and she was simply ordered to register her residence at her new address. After she received her full pardon, Eliza never committed another offence. Most of the 'crimes' she had committed in the colony were breaches of regulations that did not apply to 'free' settlers, in any case. Though her transition from British convict to law-abiding Australian citizen was not the smoothest, Eliza did manage to create a new kind of life for herself after transportation.

Unlike Eliza, Mary Leonard had been married when she was transported, and her daughter accompanied her on the voyage. Being a married mother did little to deter Mary from finding a new relationship a year after arriving in Van Diemen's Land and she bigamously married fellow convict William Holmes on 29 November 1852. Whereas Eliza was mainly punished for breaking convict regulations after arriving in Australia, Mary committed a substantive offence. She was charged with stealing money from a fellow lodger, Mrs Lyons, in 1855. It appeared that both accused and victim had been drinking rather freely, and Mary took the opportunity to pick Mrs Lyons's pocket. She was sentenced to twelve months' custody to be served in Launceston prison. When she was being escorted to Launceston by Constable Haines, both Mary and Constable Haines arrived in town blind drunk. Mary received another three months for 'being under the influence' of alcohol.

In 1858 she received her ticket-of-leave, and the following year she received her conditional pardon. The same year she committed an assault and criminal damage when she broke her neighbour's windows and door. This was after Mary and her friend had drunk two quarts of beer together, and then had a fight. She continued to offend, and was also a victim of crime herself, being hit on the head with a stone by a neighbour in 1864. Then, in 1868, the local newspaper reported that,

> A woman named Mary Leonard, about 40 years of age, residing at New Town, dropped down dead. She was a married woman, and had been under medical treatment for some time, complaining of a pain in her chest and side, and palpitation of the heart. At the time of her death she was driving some geese, when she suddenly fell down. Her husband carried her into the house where she died in his arms.

Mary and Eliza offended together, were transported to Australia together, and were only separated when they arrived in Van Diemen's Land. Mary remained in the south of Tasmania whilst Eliza went up north to Launceston. In many ways they continued to live similar lives but, whilst Eliza was able to (eventually) leave offending behind, Mary continued to get into trouble for a long time after she had been transported. Similar women, having similar experiences, still ended their lives very differently.

Chapter 13

ELLEN DWYER AND LOTTIE CHILD

(B. 1854 GALWAY AND 1865 STAFFS) – HABITUAL OFFENDERS

Ellen Dwyer's life as an offender is remarkable for its unremarkableness. She was caught up in a cycle of offending, prison and reoffending again which seemed to affect women much more than it did men. As such she was typical of thousands of women who committed relatively minor crimes, and who were seen to be a nuisance that the courts dealt with by imposing ineffective short prison sentences. We do not know when Ellen's offending cycle started as she grew up in Ireland and only emigrated to England (and into records we can access) when she was nearly 30 years old.

In 1881, Ellen was living in Wolstanton, with her husband Samuel, who was a miner, and her children. They were all living with Samuel's brother, and altogether there were twelve people living in that small Staffordshire house. She seems to have led an honest life for the next seven years, and then started to offend on a regular basis. Perhaps some crisis had befallen the family in the late 1880s, or possibly the marriage had broken down, or her husband had died in one of the frequent mining accidents that plagued the trade. The records show that Ellen committed her first offence in April 1888 when she was convicted for stealing dresses at Tunstall in Stoke-on-Trent. Although it was her first conviction, she was sentenced to go to prison for two months. Two years later she was again convicted of stealing, this time it was shirts in Hanley, Stoke-on-Trent, and this resulted in another

71

Mother and child.

short prison sentence. In fact she was convicted three times, and imprisoned three times, just in that one year. In 1891 she received six months in Stafford Prison for stealing an apron; and another nine months in the same prison the following year for stealing another shirt.

For the next three years, Ellen was convicted of stealing a basket, some aprons, some ham, a shawl, bed sheets and other bits of clothing. Though her sentences each time were only short, they added up to long periods of time spent in prison. She then stole a pair of boots and, instead of going off to the local magistrates, she was sent to Staffordshire Quarter Sessions, and there she was sentenced to three years in Stafford Prison. That was in November 1904, and after release she was quickly reconvicted again of stealing shirts and given another three-year sentence in January 1907. For her eighteenth conviction, she was given six months at Chester Assizes for stealing clothes at Crewe, at which point we lose touch with Ellen. By this time she had assumed a number of aliases – Ellen McGuire, Margaret Mulley, Margaret Dwyer – and possibly she had even more, so she becomes difficult to isolate and trace in the records. Ellen, like many offenders who did not want to be found, has 'given us the slip'.

Lottie Child's life was similar to Ellen's in many ways. She also had aliases, and was first convicted as Lottie Gallon in Liverpool. She had stolen a valuable item (a watch) so might have considered herself lucky to get off with just three months' custody. As Lottie Callaghan she was living with her husband and two daughters in West Derby, Liverpool, in 1891. Like Ellen, Lottie had a period where she was not before the courts, and it was only in 1896 that she began a cycle of reoffending. In that year, Lottie was twice convicted of theft at Hanley and served two short prison sentences; and another three the following year for minor offences. In 1899 she was given three months for stealing sheets in the name of Lottie Marion Buckley. The same year she was convicted in the name of Lottie Gallon of helping her first-born daughter, Mary, to escape from a reformatory school (Mary must have been placed there after committing a crime as a youth). Back again as Lottie Buckley she was convicted of stealing blankets at Birkenhead. Then she was convicted at Chester Quarter Sessions for stealing dress material in the name of Lottie Childs, for which she received six months' hard labour. Records indicate that she continued to offend until at least 1910, and then, just like Ellen, Lottie's paper trail runs cold too. The sad postscript to Lottie's tale is that we do know that another of her daughters, also called Lottie, was placed into a reformatory school in Hertford in 1911. Without luck, a lot of support and personal resilience, she was in danger of following in her mother's footsteps. Lottie and Ellen shared similar offending patterns – committing minor thefts and receiving lots of short prison sentences. They also shared the same limited life opportunities. Once they had been imprisoned once or twice they would have lost their good name, reduced their chances of securing employment and often alienated their families (at a time when extended families often gave crucial financial and emotional support). In Ellen's case it may be that the family had already broken up by the time she started to commit offences; for Lottie, although her husband seems never to have offended, her daughters were caught up in a disruptive childhood, and faced their own troubles early in their lives.

Both Lottie and Ellen were typical of a large number of women who never committed 'serious enough' crimes to be sent to penal servitude for a number of years, but who repeatedly served short prison sentences which blighted their lives for just as long as a spell in a convict prison. They never got back on their feet when they left local prisons, and both led 'stuttering' lives of being 'on the outside', and back again to being 'on the inside', with prison defining their lives to a large extent.

Chapter 14

EMILY SWANN

(B. 1860 CAWTHORNE, YORKS) – EXECUTED

Emily Hinchcliffe was born the daughter of a miner in Cawthorne near Barnsley in 1860. She married glassblower William Swann in Silkstone, York, when she was 21, and they moved into a house in Ardsley, near Barnsley. They had a large family, with children born in 1883, 1885, 1886, 1891, 1894, 1897, 1899 and 1901. They may have had another child in 1892, Emily Swann, possibly named after her mother, but the records are not good enough to be conclusive. That child died aged six months following a vaccination. The Coroner at Stainfoot, near Ardsley, stated that the child had not died from the vaccination, but from poison being put into the child sometime afterwards, with no explanation or evidence as to how that poison had been administered. No one was ever charged in connection with the death of this child.

In 1901, Emily, her husband and their lodger, John Gallagher, were living in Wombwell, a small village near Barnsley. The 1903 'Wombwell Murders' were reported in *The Times* and *Daily Mail*, but most of the information on the case comes from the local newspapers. They described Emily as a stumpy little, round-faced woman, 4 foot 10 inches tall and 122lbs in weight and from a 'respectable' background'. When Emily was 42, the 30-year-old Gallagher was stated to be a sympathetic friend. The newspapers described a tumultuous household, with William beating Emily on several occasions, although no cases for domestic violence were ever pursued in the courts. Whether John was the cause of the problems or not, and it seems likely that Emily and John enjoyed a close relationship, he had resolved to leave Wombwell for Barnsley in June 1903. However, events overtook him.

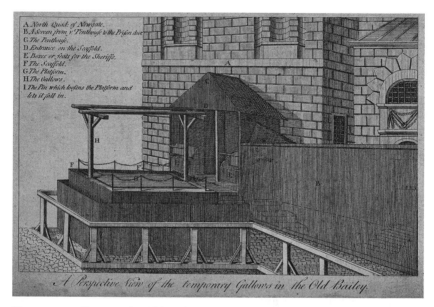

A North Quad of Newgate.
B. A Screen from y' Penthouse to the Prison door
C. The Penthouse.
D. Entrance on the Scaffold.
E. Boxes or Seats for the Sheriffs.
F The Scaffold.
G The Platform.
H The Gallows.
I The Pin which loosens the Platform and lets it fall in.

A Perspective View of the temporary Gallows in the Old Bailey.

Temporary gallows at the Old Bailey.

On 6 June Emily arrived at her neighbour's house with a shawl over her head, two black-eyes, and bruises on her face. On seeing the injuries caused by Emily's husband, John Gallagher said, 'I'll go and give him something for himself for that.' The neighbours witnessed him going to confront William Swann, closely followed by Emily. John was reported to have shouted, 'I'll coffin him before morning.' There was a prolonged fight in the Swann's house, at the end of which John emerged stating, 'I've busted four of his ribs and I'll bust four more'. Resting for a few minutes, he then told his neighbours, 'I'll finish him out before I go to Bradford. I'll murder the pig before morning. If he can't kick a man he shan't kick a woman.' He re-entered the Swanns' house and accompanied by a shout of 'Give it to him, Johnny' from Emily, another fight ensued. When John and Emily came out of the house again, holding hands and reportedly looking affectionately at each other, William was lying fatally injured with head wounds on the floor. Indeed, Emily calmly informed her neighbours that her husband was now dead.

The police arrived and Emily was arrested immediately. John went on the run for two months, living rough and staying with relatives in Middlesbrough before he was apprehended. John and Emily were tried at Leeds Assizes in October 1903. Their defence advocate wove a narrative which suggested they were guilty of manslaughter if anything. However, in directing the jury, the judge in the case gave his opinion that John's remark, 'I'll finish him out before I go to Bradford' showed that there was intent to commit murder. 'As for the woman' he continued, 'it is my duty to tell you that one does not commit murder only with one's hands. If one person instigates another to commit murder, and that other person does it, the instigator is also guilty of murder.' After one hour's deliberation, the jury returned a verdict of 'guilty' on both parties.

When the damning verdict was announced, Emily stated, 'I am innocent. I am not afraid of immediate death, because I am innocent and will go to God.' The judge then pronounced a capital sentence, and Emily smiled and blew a kiss to someone in the gallery as she was led down from the dock.

Emily and John were taken from the court to Armley Prison, Leeds, where they were placed in separate condemned cells. The only time Emily and John saw each other between sentence and execution was at the prison chapel service on Christmas morning where they were kept separate and not allowed to speak. They reportedly both ate a substantial Christmas dinner, but there is no real evidence of that, and it was likely just press speculation and gossip. In an article entitled 'Awaiting Their Doom', *the Daily Mail* reported that Emily was suffering with depression and insomnia. She repeatedly told her female warders that she was concerned about the disgrace she was bringing on her family. Emily's family did make one last appeal for clemency, but the Home Secretary declined to interfere.

A few minutes before 8 o'clock on the morning of Tuesday, 29 December 1903, Emily had a glass of brandy in her cell, was escorted to the place of execution where she said, 'Good morning' to John Gallagher, who was already covered with a hood. He replied, 'Good morning love.' The noose was then placed around her neck, and her last words were, 'Good-bye. God bless you.' The autopsy found that death was instantaneous for both Emily and John.

Chapter 15

ELIZABETH DILLON

(B. 1844 BIRMINGHAM) – CONVICT

Elizabeth Dillon was born in 1844. Her parents Michael and Catherine were both migrants from County Roscommon in Ireland, and she was the youngest of seven children. The Dillons lived on the poverty line. Elizabeth was already working in Birmingham's industrial centre by the age of 7, assisting her three sisters at a pin-making factory where her small hands were invaluable for attaching the heads to pins.

When she was 16, her father, Michael, died. For many families, the loss of a male breadwinner was not only a personal loss, but a financial crisis too. Sons and daughters were often driven to extreme levels to try and keep the family afloat. Elizabeth's seems to have been one such case. It was less than a year after the death of her father that Elizabeth began working as a prostitute.

By 1862 Elizabeth was working the streets and using the name Elizabeth Lamb. Clearly struggling to adjust to her mode of living she began frequenting pubs on a daily basis, and developed a 'robust' attitude. On one occasion when asked to leave a pub after insulting many customers and striking one drinker in the face, she went outside and smashed several windowpanes. Elizabeth begun to be known in Birmingham as a 'disorderly character', and she occasionally worked in a brothel rather than tramping the streets looking for business. There she was befriended by older women in the trade, and schooled in the art of picking the pockets of customers.

Elizabeth's life on the street saw her come into conflict not only with the police and members of the public, but with other prostitutes too. Rowing over places to ply their trade, customers, insults, money

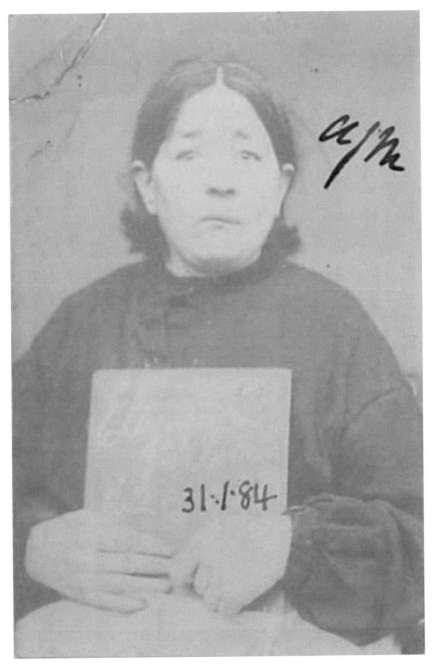

Elizabeth Dillon. Courtesy of TNA, PCOM4; Piece: 57; Item: 9.

and drink, fighting prostitutes posed multiple affronts to social sensibilities. Though fights could be violent, both women would usually find themselves charged with public order, rather than bodily harm, offences. In 1868 for example, Elizabeth was arrested for fighting with Mary Ann Blackman. Both were imprisoned, not for the damage they did to one another, but for the use of obscene language, and causing a disturbance in a public thoroughfare.

The following year, 1869, Elizabeth bore a son, George. Elizabeth's pregnancy may have been the unwanted result of her work as a prostitute, or from a personal relationship. However, the name of George's father was never disclosed on any official document. Elizabeth and George moved into another common lodging house, and Elizabeth continued to seek factory work and supplement her earnings through prostitution. The birth of an illegitimate child was always a challenge to women, for Elizabeth who had been living so long on the margins of society, and of destitution, it can only have intensified her plight.

By the early 1880s Elizabeth had been convicted more than forty times. She had been taken to the police court for riotous behaviour, drunkenness and disorderly conduct, obscene language, vagrancy, wilful damage, prostitution, theft, and assault. Her sentences were usually between one week and two months in length, and she had spent a combined total of more than five years in prison.

It could be very difficult for offenders like Elizabeth to judge what the penalty for any given crime was going to be. On one occasion drunkenness or riotous behaviour might earn a woman seven days in prison, on another three months. The same could be said of theft. Whilst most offenders were aware the penalty for property crimes was higher than those of violence or public order, theft could also be punished with as small an imprisonment as obscene language. In October 1883, for example, Elizabeth spent a single month in prison for the theft of a pair of boots. It must have come as a surprise to her months later when, in 1884, the theft of a pair of trousers from Rosina Ash was met with a sentence of five years' penal servitude.

Much of Elizabeth's time in prison was characterised by ill-health, and she was regularly found to be incapable of carrying out prison labour, something prison authorities usually only allowed to the seriously incapacitated. Her conduct in prison was good, and Elizabeth was released from Woking Prison in 1887. She was given a train ticket back to Birmingham. When she arrived she almost immediately entered the workhouse. It is not clear where her son was taken on her arrest three years earlier, or whether the two were ever reunited after her release.

After a brief respite from offending, and time to recover from the illness that had plagued her in prison, Elizabeth returned to the streets of Birmingham and to the chaos of her former life. In October 1893 Elizabeth was brought to court for breaking twelve panes of glass belonging to her neighbour, Maria Smith. Elizabeth admitted the offence, and complained that Maria had cheated her out of a shilling and sixpence. When told she would be going to prison, Elizabeth declared that when she came out again, she would break the rest of Maria's windows. The clerk cautioned her, and reminded her that she had been before the court a total of fifty-four times, to which Elizabeth replied 'Yes, dirty 'Ria, and I'll make it sixty times for you, you old cat.' Elizabeth was then removed from the dock screaming abuse.

Lives like Elizabeth's were, ultimately, unsustainable. Due to her chaotic lifestyle and frequent moves Elizabeth had no network of friends and family to support her as she aged. She had not had stable work since her childhood in Birmingham's factories. Even in the most favourable circumstances, as women aged, their options for formal and informal work decreased. The older women got, the harder and less well paid even prostitution became. Elizabeth had attempted to work as a hawker, but evidently did not turn enough profit to support herself. By 1901, at the age of 57, Elizabeth was back living in the workhouse, where she died five years later.

Chapter 16

EVA BEBBINGTON

(B. 1901 CREWE) – RESCUE HOME

Eva Bebbington was born in Crewe (then commonly known as Monks Coppenhall) in 1901. Her parents, William and Sarah Jane, were not strangers to the courts. Her father William was charged and convicted of drunkenness, not paying rates and for not paying for services. He was also convicted under the 1870 Education Acts for not regularly sending his children to school. He also found himself in trouble when his sons, Eva's brothers, were found guilty of theft and sent to Bradwall Reformatory School in Cheshire. William failed to pay a contribution towards their being kept in the reform school, and he was back before the courts, being forced to pay his contribution and also a fine. During his lifetime William would be convicted twenty-seven times in Crewe Magistrates Courts. Eva's start in life was chaotic to say the least, with a father who was employed, but who liked to spend his money on drink, and parents who did not send their children to school. Eva's parents struggled to keep their head above water, and sometimes failed to look after their children as well as they should. Indeed, the state stepped in to look after their children on many occasions – four of their children were sent to reform school (two girls, two boys).

At just 7 years old, in 1908, Eva was convicted of theft at Crewe Magistrates' Court. She was sent to a local reform school until she was 12 years old. The magistrates may have felt they were taking Eva away from a poor family environment, since magistrates in this period often imposed long periods of separation for children from their parents if they felt the child was vulnerable. They may have

Former rescue home, Vicar's Lane, Chester.

been wise to do so in this case since after Eva returned to the family home there was a disturbing report in the local newspapers.

On 15 July 1916, the *Crewe Chronicle* headline announced a 'Sordid Story at Crewe. Young Girl's Serious Plight':

> Supt. Thompson said that the case was one of a very serious nature, Eva Bebbington being only 15 years and four months old. She had pleaded guilty. She had been on remand since Friday with a view to her being got into a suitable home. He had been in communication with Miss Wright of Chester, and that lady had expressed herself willing to take her, and the girl was willing to go with her. They wished to save her if possible, and give her a chance of leading a new life ... The parents of Eva Bebbington were charged with conducing to their daughter's offence by their negligence and drunken habits. The police had found it necessary to go to the house and warn them. This young girl (Eva Bebbington) was out at night as late as 12 o'clock and 2 o'clock in the morning, and the parents were of such drunken habits that they could not possibly exercise proper care over her. The father had been

before the court 27 times for various offences and the mother twice for neglect of family. Both had had three months for neglect and the mother in addition 21 days … Serg. Lythgoe said that on Thursday night he was in Nantwich Road. He saw Eva Bebbington and she accosted several soldiers. She went away with one to Gresty Road. He followed and told the man the girl's age. He arrested her and took her to the police station and charged her. She made no reply … PC Hardy said he had seen the girl Eva Bebbington out late at night. When passing the parents' house he had heard drunken rows and disorderliness. He did not think they exercised reasonable care over their child. He had seen the girl at the railway station. When he served the summons, the mother said 'I will go on my holidays after this'.

In fact, despite being found guilty and threatening the police witness during the trial, she did not go to prison for her part in the offence, and neither did William. Both were fined 40s. (this equated to about two weeks' wages for a slater like William). At the age of 15, Eva was sent to Miss Wright's Rescue home for three years. The moral education she received was designed to put her back 'on the straight and narrow' and, importantly, reduce the influence her parents had over her life. Eva would also have received some basic education, and some employment training which would be of practical benefit to her when she was allowed to leave (aged 17).

After Eva left the Rescue Home in 1919, she becomes very difficult to track in the records, since 1911 is the last available census in which to find her. Moreover, in a period when women changed their surname on marriage, it becomes much more difficult to trace women in historical records. For example, three different women named Eva Bebbington were married in Nantwich between 1916 and 1928. It is unlikely that the 1916 marriage was 'our' Eva (although it is not completely out of the question), but either of the other two marriage records (to Evan Edwards and to George Morris) could relate to her. The good news for Eva is that there were no other cases against anyone called Eva Bebbington, Eva Morris or Eva Edwards, in Crewe Magistrates Courts, apart for an unlicensed dog case in 1936. So, Eva seems to have steered clear of any serious offending after her experience in Miss Wright's Home. Perhaps she gained employment, a good marriage and a settled family life, which all helped her to reform and lead a better and healthier life than her parents before her.

Chapter 17

JULIA SMITH AND FRANCES MURPHY

(B. 1865 CREWE AND 1869 LIVERPOOL) – EARLY DEATHS

Born without the ability to either speak or hear, Julia Smith faced a hard life. She was born in 1865 and lived with her parents and siblings in Crewe (Church Coppenhall). Aged 15 she was working as a domestic servant in 1881, but by 1883 she had been convicted of vagrancy, probably for being homeless. Her father died two years later in 1885 (when he was 50 years old), the year she was first convicted of prostitution. Prostitution itself was not illegal, but court registers often recorded the offence as 'prostitution' if the defendant was assumed to make her living in that way – the real offence that Julia committed may have been vagrancy, public obscenity or urination, or soliciting for business. She was convicted four more times in the next six years, once for drunkenness, twice for vagrancy and once again for prostitution. And then her, difficult and probably quite unhappy short life was brought to a sudden end when she died in 1891, aged just 36.

Frances Murphy was born four years after Julia, in Liverpool. Her family moved to Crewe in 1889 but she obviously still liked to spend time in her home town, as she was convicted of drunkenness in Liverpool in 1890. She already had twenty-two convictions by this time, mainly for drunkenness and disorderliness, but here were also four felonies (more serious offences heard on indictment at a Quarter Sessions Court rather than the local magistrates' court). When Frances then stole a jacket belonging to her landlady in Crewe, she again ran back to Liverpool (where she was arrested). Once out of prison, she

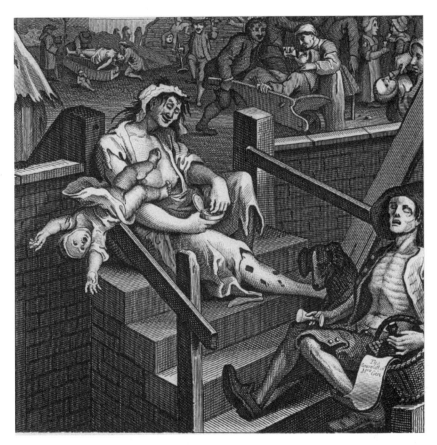

William Hogarth's Gin Lane *1751.*

was convicted of drunkenness and prostitution, but also a prosecuted for a string of assaults, all in 1891. She was acquitted of the assault on another woman, Sarah Ellis, but convicted of assaulting a man, and received two months' custody. She was then reconvicted for a more serious offence. This time it was for grievous bodily harm on a 10-year-old child whom she had hit on the head with a bottle. She received another two-month prison sentence. During her trial Frances had threatened to 'swing for' one of the witnesses, but she never got the chance. She died in 1893 aged just 24.

Just because we have a couple of examples of prostitutes who died young does not show that prostitution shortened one's life. Many working and poor women died early from leading an unhealthy and physically demanding life. Nevertheless, earning money in this risky way, a choice few women would have made lightly, not only involved the risk of violence or catching diseases such as syphilis or venereal disease, it also meant spending long periods outside in cold weather, sleeping in stinking alleyways, picking up 'normal' diseases from clients and so on. It could wear a body out very quickly.

Chapter 18

MARIA ALLEN AND MARIA ADAMS

(B. 1808 AND 1862) – CONVICTS

When the census was taken in 1881 it revealed that the youngest woman in a convict prison was Maria Adams, aged 17. She had been sentenced to five years' penal service in 1879 for stealing clothes. That was her fifth conviction, having first been convicted at Birmingham for a similar theft, aged 15.

When she entered Millbank Prison her health was recorded as 'good' except for a small wound on her forehead, and that her weight was 122lbs, so the authorities considered her to be 'fat'. Her record in Woking also noted that she was 'very excitable and easily influenced by other prisoners to do acts of violence though she is not naturally of bad disposition'. She did, however, manage to rack up a large number of breaches for prison indiscipline. She was punished for refusing to walk during the exercise period, breaking panes of glass in her cell (thirty on one occasion), using obscene language, striking and biting male officers and using disgusting language to officers when she was removed to the punishment cell for solitary confinement.

On 5 May 1881 she was found to be 'Making signs to prisoners in D Hall, and when checked [told off] threatening to use violence against Assist. Matron O'Connor, and for rushing at the Officer named, striking her violently on the head, pulling her hair, and swearing she would take her life.' She was sent to Millbank for her punishment, which was a reduced diet, losing remission, which meant the date she was eligible for early release was pushed back, and serving eighteen days in solitary confinement. After

Maria Adams. Courtesy of TNA, PCOM4; Piece: 57; Item: 9.

Maria Allen. Courtesy of TNA, PCOM4; Piece: 72; Item: 7.

her punishment Maria was sent to Fulham, where she was then punished for 'putting herself in a black temper', threatening fellow prisoners, officers and saying that she would take her own life. She was punished for breaching prison regulations eighteen times in 1881, three in 1882, six in 1883 and three in 1884. Either she became reconciled to her situation, or the system ground her down and she resisted less and less as the years passed by. That was, of course, part of the function of such tight control over convicts in the prison estate. Women were held to a higher standard than male prisoners, with obscene language or indecorous unfeminine behaviour being harshly punished.

Maria sent letters to her mother every six months, care of Maria's stepfather. He was Abraham Clarke, who had married her mother Mary when Maria was 2 years old. The police report on Abraham stated that he was 'a respectable man with good character'. When Maria was released on conditional licence on 15 Aug 1884, she was discharged to her mother and stepfather's address in Aston Manor, Birmingham. Because of the number of infringements that Maria had committed inside prison, the early release date had been pushed back to a point where she only had two months more to serve when she walked out of the prison gates.

We do not know for how long Maria lived with her mother and stepfather. She was still young when she was released and she may have subsequently got married (changing her surname), or she might have moved away under an alias; either way it would be difficult to trace her after that point. She never appeared under the name Maria Adams in the Criminal Registers, so hopefully Maria matured out of her criminal career, and led a happy life.

Maria Allen had served a number of years' custody by the time Maria Adams was born. She had launched into a significant criminal career relatively late in her life. She was first convicted of larceny in 1852 when she was 44. She went into custody for six months; and another twelve months in 1854. Almost as soon as she got out, she was convicted of larceny again, and sentenced to four years' penal servitude. She received another five years for stealing sheets in 1861 and was released on licence in 1865. She intended to go to the London Discharged Prisoners' Aid Society. They would provide some temporary shelter for her, and some practical help. They could even help to find ex-convicts some employment.

Described as a widow with two children in 1867, Maria was convicted of stealing a coat at Middlesex Quarter Sessions, and she was sentenced to penal servitude for seven years. She was released into the care of Battery House Refuge on 23 November 1871. Just over a year later she was back in court, again for larceny, this time for stealing three coats. Another seven years penal servitude was imposed. The long prison sentences did not appear to be having any effect on her, however. In 1880 she stole another sheet, and at the age of 72 she received a ten-year sentence at Surrey Sessions. She was sent to Millbank, then to Woking Female Prison, until she was released on conditional licence in March 1887. She again went back to the Discharged Prisoners' Aid Society for help when she was finally released.

Since she was first convicted at the age of 44, Maria Allen had spent thirty-two years in convict prisons, and she was the oldest female convict when the 1881 census was taken. There was a difference of nearly fifty years between the two Marias, but the system would take anyone over the age of 14 until very old age. It made very little allowance for the infirm, the comparatively young and inexperienced or the aged. The system pressed down on them all, distinguishing only between those who followed the rules, and those who broke them.

Chapter 19

MARY ANN PARR

(B. 1830 DERBYSHIRE) – BROADMOOR NO. 1

Mary Ann Parr was described in the 1851 census as a 'blind pauper inmate' of Bingham's 200-bed workhouse. That had been her home since she was a teenager, and indeed she was one of the first inmates after it opened in 1837. Mary was still living in the workhouse when the *Nottinghamshire Guardian* reported that:

> The greatest excitement was occasioned in the village of Bingham last week by the announcement that a murder of a very revolting description had been committed in the Union Workhouse – the criminal being a female inmate called Mary Ann Parr, the victim her illegitimate female child. The unnatural mother appeared to have resolved upon destroying her unfortunate infant and from the time of its birth had refused to give it the breast, and neglected and ill-treated, and … by the wretched woman's own confession, had wilfully murdered it … [a fellow inmate stated] She had not prepared for it, would not say who the father was … she had plenty of milk for the child, but would not let it suck. We had to put the child to her breast by force. I told her Monday last that if it did not suck it would die. She replied 'Let it die'.

Several women from the workhouse deposed that Mary was sane, that she was warned about smothering the baby, and that she had confessed to her crime shortly afterwards. The surgeon was not

Sampson Kempthorne's workhouse design as illustrated in Poor Law Commissioners, Annual Report, *vol. 1, (1835), p. 411.*

convinced the child had been deliberately smothered but Mary confessed: 'I did smother the child against my breast. I took the child to my breast at first to suckle it. I then squeezed it against my breast on purpose to take away its life, and when I saw it was dead I was frightened. I was not exactly sure it was dead till my mistress told me'.

The *Derby Mercury* further explained that,

> The prisoner is a woman of an exceedingly low development, and her blindness gives an expression to the countenance of extreme silliness. She unites with her apparent craziness,

however, a low cunning, and, when she found that the law was likely to execute justice, she made an attempt to scale the workhouse wall and escape – a design which she failed to consummate.

She was tried at Nottingham Assizes on 3 March 1853, and found guilty of the wilful murder of her ten-day-old daughter. Despite the ruthless treatment she received from the press, there was considerable sympathy at this time for women who had been forced into desperate acts through poverty, or, as seemed to be the case with Mary, through mental inadequacy. Mary was sentenced to death, but her mental condition was such that her sentence was commuted to transportation for life. She was taken from the Assize Court to Nottingham Gaol. In 1863 she was removed to Broadmoor, becoming their first ever patient (Case Number 1).

After discussion which began in the 1850s and the passing of the Criminal Lunatics Act in 1860, building began on a new secure institution near Reading in Berkshire. Broadmoor accepted its first patients (including Mary Parr) in 1863. For the first year only women were resident, but men were admitted from 1864. The original building plan of five blocks for men and one for women was completed in 1868. Over its lifetime, men would outnumber women at Broadmoor by about four to one in the Victorian period; men also served longer periods of time in the hospital, and had a greater chance of dying there. Whereas one in three women were discharged before death, only one in five men would be discharged before they died in Broadmoor.

The Broadmoor Admission register stated that Mary was:

> Suicidal. Believes that everybody is her enemy. Constantly dreaming of murders. Complains of pains in her head and is most obstinate and intractable disposition. No education. Temperate. Church of England.

Nearly thirty-years later, the notes made by Dr Orange, the Superintendent of Broadmoor Hospital, noted that Mary was

Much enfeebled. Occasionally irritable, quarrelsome and excited. Present state indifferent. She is mentally unsound. Not suitable for workhouse, having been 32 years in Bethel and Broadmoor. No friends.

She died in Broadmoor at 4.55am, 31 July 1900, of chronic kidney disease. She had been kept in Broadmoor for forty-seven years.

There was a rather tragic post-script to Mary's story. The Broadmoor files have a copy of a letter sent by her nephew. It said:

Dear Aunt, please excuse my long delay in writing I assure you it is not because I do not think of you which I often do it is so long since I heard from you that I do want to know how you are getting on an I shall be glad to hear from you as soon as possible, the years keep passing and I begin to feel that I am getting on in life ... Please write soon and think of me has your ever-loving Nephew.

By the time the letter fell through Broadmoor's letter box, Mary had been dead for nearly two years.

Chapter 20

MARY HARDYMAN

(B. 1829 GALWAY) – CONVICT NO. 4344

Mary, her husband Michael, and her unmarried sister-in-law, were an Irish family from Galway living in Malt Shovel Yard in York in 1851. By 1861 they had moved on to live in Middlesbrough, and their household now had three children as well. Ten years later they were back in Yorkshire: Michael found work as a labourer, and Mary became a spinner working in one of Bradford's many worsted factories. Mary would have been earning about 20s. a week as a factory worker in this period, which would have enabled a reasonable standard of living, and some measure of independence. Her life does not seem to have been quiet and free of trouble in this period though.

In 1875, there was a report in the local newspaper:

> A Brutal Fellow … Dennis Hardyman, of Black Bull Lane, Walmgate, was summonsed for having violently assaulted his mother, Mary Hardyman. The defendant did not answer the summons, and it was stated that when it was served upon him, he laughed …The alleged assault was that the defendant, at twelve o'clock at night, dragged his mother out of bed by the hair and attempted to throw her into the street. A variety of convictions were proved against him dating as far back at 1864 and it was also stated that the defendant had been a soldier and was dismissed from the service owing to his bad conduct. … He was committed to York castle for two months.

Mary Hardyman. Courtesy of TNA PCOM4; Piece: 68; Item: 5.

Mary was again a victim of assault the following year when her neighbour, Bridget Bane, struck her with a poker. However, she also committed acts of violence herself:

> Assault on a Soldier … Mary Hardyman, a well-known character, was charged with assaulting Henry Birkenshaw, a recruiting sergeant residing at the York barracks. … defendant had been five times previously before the bench, was fined 20s and costs.

This is a revealing piece of information. Although there are no newspaper reports, and the convict prison licence does not record them, Mary had clearly been before the courts a number of times – although we are left to guess the offences she was accused of, possibly, given her offending record over the next few years, they were alcohol-related or involved theft.

In July 1878, the newspapers had further news of Mary: 'An Impudent Thief … Mary Hardyman, married woman, of Walmgate, was charged with stealing a piece of beef … at the time she was worse for drink'. Mary was imprisoned for one month at York Castle Gaol for this offence. Then a couple of months later she was back in the prison, this time for stealing a basket from a wagon left unguarded in her old place of residence (Malt Shovel Yard). This time sentence was harsher; the courts imposed an eighteen-month prison sentence followed by four years' police supervision.

Not long after she was released, her husband Michael died and was buried in York. A year later Mary was sentenced by Quarter Sessions judges at York to five years' penal servitude, and another four years' police supervision when she was released from convict prison. Her crime had been stealing another piece of meat. We do not know what Mary's state of health was when she was admitted to custody. The record shows that she had a sallow complexion, light brown hair, blue eyes, 5 feet 3 inches tall, proportionate build, oval face. She had scars over her right temple, her left-side upper lip. Her ears were pierced and she was missing several teeth. However, she also had underlying health problems. The prison record states that she was excused all hard prison labour due to her weak lungs. She was then treated in the hospital infirmary for heart disease between 8 January and 16 March 1885. She was well enough to go back to the prison wings until she was released on conditional licence one year and eight months early in July 1886. By that time she had served more than half of her prison sentence. The record states that she left prison to live with her son, the ex-soldier with whom she had previously had such a problematic relationship, in Providence Square, Walmsgate. However, with a history of ill-health she did not have much time to enjoy her freedom. She died eighteen months after release from Woking Prison.

Chapter 21

ELIZABETH DYER

(B. 1824 LONDON) – TRANSPORTED

It was second time unlucky for Elizabeth Webb when she appeared at the Old Bailey and was sentenced to seven years' transportation in August 1850 for stealing a watch, guard and 8s. from Thomas Jebb.

Jebb contended that he had met Elizabeth in the Red Lion pub in Greenwich, and that as he had sat with her she had complained to him of poverty and hunger. Jebb said that he bought her a drink and passed a few hours with Elizabeth before going home. When he got up to leave, Elizabeth followed him home, and went upstairs with him, lying on the bed. When he woke up in the morning, he missed his watch and chain from the bedside table and 8s. in cash. The inference in Jebb's testimony was that Elizabeth was a prostitute, with whom he had spent the night, but who had robbed him as he slept and made her escape.

Elizabeth denied the charge when she was apprehended, and was found to have 8s. in her possession, but no watch. Elizabeth denied the accusation of prostitution, although this was almost certainly true. She had been living in common lodging houses.

The case against Elizabeth was compounded when a police constable produced a certificate which showed Elizabeth had a previous conviction. In 1848, Elizabeth had entered a Deptford shop with her friend Catherin Ganey and stolen a pair of boots. They had tried to use the boots to pay their landlady in lieu of rent, but had soon been found out and turned over to the police. Although she had only broken the law once before, and for minor theft, Elizabeth's

Sketch of Hobart Town by Edward Carlton Booth 1873.

record spoke against her, gaining her a punishment that would irrevocably alter her life.

Elizabeth joined Susannah Wells, Eliza Conner and Mary Leonard aboard the *Emma Eugenia,* and arrived in Van Diemen's Land in 1851. Elizabeth was just 26 when she sailed and she was married to Thomas, a labourer, with whom she had four young children. Elizabeth would never see her family again.

Upon arrival in Australia, Elizabeth did not settle into the convict regime easily. She was punished a number of times for talking out of turn and disobedience while she was held on probation awaiting assignment. When she was posted out to private households, she proved equally challenging. She absconded six months after arrival whilst in the service of a Mr Stokell. She was quickly apprehended, but absconded again the following month. Seven months later, whilst being transported on a steamer, Elizabeth escaped again, and she absconded the following year whilst in the service of a Mr Moses.

Elizabeth was challenging authority in other ways too. Despite still being legally married to her husband back in England, Elizabeth applied to marry Thomas Brown, a free settler, in 1851. Permission was granted, but Brown died the following year. Soon after, Elizabeth applied to marry again. This time, her intended was Edward Stephen Dyer, a convict from Wiltshire, transported for fifteen years for stabbing a police constable. Edward had arrived on the *John Calvin* in 1847, and was granted his ticket-of-leave in 1853. Her first two applications to marry Dyer were turned down, presumably on account of her poor behaviour under sentence, but her third attempt was successful. It seems incredible that a convict who made not one, but four applications to marry bigamously was never detected. Yet with imperfect records of a convict's history, it was not as uncommon as we might expect for convicts to contract new marriages. For many, their former lives on the other side of the world must have seemed much less real than the new people and opportunities being presented to them in the colony. When Elizabeth received her own ticket-of-leave in 1854, the pair married almost immediately. They went on to have five children together: Edward, Charles, Mary, Sarah and Elizabeth – making Elizabeth a mother of nine surviving children.

Elizabeth would have been considered one of transportation's success stories. She was never reconvicted. However, Edward found himself several times in trouble. In 1856 Edward absconded (he still had five years of his sentence unexpired) to Victoria, along with thousands of other convicts and free settlers seeking to make their fortunes following the discovery of gold. In the year Edward travelled to Victoria, almost 95,000 kilograms of gold were found by diggers. Edward returned some time later and the family settled to life in Hobart, although they found it a less bountiful place than other convict families. In 1862, Elizabeth and Edward were both in court, but for a civil dispute with their landlord. The landlord alleged that the Dyers owed six months' rent, but Elizabeth and Edward contended that they were within their rights to refuse payment due to the dire state of the house to which the landlord refused to make any repairs. The case was found in their favour. However, the Dyers and their children now found themselves with nowhere to live.

Edward returned to Victoria in search of fortune again, this time taking Elizabeth and the children with him. After three years failing to find gold they returned to Hobart in January 1865. A few years later, in 1868 Edward, still struggling to find regular work, was imprisoned for being on private premises for an unlawful purpose. Even with her husband imprisoned, Elizabeth did not return to offending – perhaps all too aware how quickly a family could fall apart on account of a single conviction.

Chapter 22

MARY VICKERS ALIAS 'SLASHER'

(B. 1849 CREWE) – PROSTITUTION

Mary grew up with her parents living at Crewe Gates Farm (next to Crewe Hall) in Cheshire where her father was one of the gardeners. When she was 21 she married local railway worker Charles Vickers. A year later, in 1871, they had their first child, Clara. Everything in formal records would suggest that they were a happily married couple, however, a newspaper report in 1872 indicated that life was not so settled for the Vickers family. The article in the *Crewe Chronicle* described how a 'tipsy' neighbour, Mrs Maxwell, ran into Mary's house screaming that her husband was going to kill her. She was pursued by Mr Maxwell, and they began to fight each other in the Vickers's garden. Police Constable Clutton arrived and attempted to separate the couple, whereupon Mr Maxwell shoved the policeman backwards. He tripped over a garden ladder and everyone heard a loud 'crack'. Not very responsibly, or wisely, the Vickers and the Maxwells ran back into the house. After quarter of an hour they came out to find the officer still lying on the ground, groaning. In the assault trial against Mr Maxwell which followed, there were a number of interesting revelations. It was alleged that Mrs Maxwell 'was in the habit of getting drunk and was a nosey woman, and when in drink she would kiss men and allow them to return the compliment'. Indeed, PC Clutton was one of those men. He had been seen the previous week with his arm round Maxwell's wife. Most interestingly, it transpired that PC Clutton had been so quick to attend the quarrel between the Maxwells because he was in the area, and not in uniform. It was further revealed that he often stopped at Mary Vickers's house, as well as Maxwell's, to 'light his pipe'.

A Cruikshank cartoon depicting a prostitute, 1799.

It also seems that Mary was a drinker herself. In 1875 she was convicted of being drunk and disorderly. In the newspaper trial report, Mary was referred to as 'Slasher'; as there had been no violent cases associated with her at this stage of her life, this was probably not because she was violent, but because of an episode of public urination. After this point she was consistently referred to as 'Slasher' in newspaper reports. Later in 1875, a raid on a 'disorderly house' found Vickers with other prostitutes and a 'bully' (a pimp) together with three children aged between 3 and 8, naked, sleeping on some rags in one corner of the room. There was no glass in any of the windows in the house due to people throwing stones and bricks through the windows. It was stated in court that prostitutes from the potteries came nearly every Friday and Saturday and stayed in that house, with great rows going on at night. Neighbours could hardly sleep at night owing to the dreadful rows and quarrels going on between the men and women; shrieks of murder and obscenities were frequent. The police inspector who brought the case told the court that 'He had been through some of the lowest places in London, Liverpool and Manchester, but he had never seen anything so bad as that house.' Vickers had been found, drunk, lying on the kitchen floor with four men, who said they were there 'for a bit of a game'. She told the court that she had financially supported her family for some time by washing and being a charwoman, but now her husband and two children were living in nearby Nantwich Workhouse.

Mary had a third daughter in 1876, the same year as her father died. And she found herself back in court. Mary Vickers had hit a neighbour's child, and the child's mother, Susannah Price, was remonstrating with Mary in the street. The women rolled over on the ground, and Price never got up. Her face was black and foaming around her mouth. She was dead. Originally charged as manslaughter, the Grand Jury threw the case out and dismissed it when the medical report stated that the woman had died of a 'fit', and that it was impossible to say if the fight had brought it on.

Over the next twelve years Mary continued to live with her husband and children (having another two children in 1885 and 1887). She also continued to be prosecuted for vagrancy, drunkenness and for 'prowling' in Chester High Street. She was variously described as a prostitute, a tramp and an old offender. Suddenly, in 1889, aged 40, she died.

Her widowed husband then looked after the children. He clearly struggled with this new role, and he was convicted for not sending the children to school in the year that Mary died. However, Charles found his feet, and got employment as a brickyard labourer. The first-born child, Clara, became a servant, so too did Elizabeth. The third daughter Agnes, got married in 1899. Charles then moved in with the newly-weds. George became a stable boy and Charles became a cow-hand. The youngest son, Charles junior, got a job in Crewe Railway Works in 1913, shortly before his father died.

It may seem remarkable that Mary, a woman who had many episodes of drunkenness, and who made money through prostitution, seems to have been able to participate in family life for so long. Despite prison sentences, living away in brothels and participating in risky behaviour, Charles and Mary raised a number of children, all of whom found employment, and made relationships themselves. Prostitution raised an income for the family when the alternative was the workhouse, and although it brought Mary into bad company, bad habits, public disrepute and into gaol, it could be seen as a reasonable choice for Mary to make. Not the wisest perhaps, but a realistic one for a woman in her position.

Chapter 23

SARAH CHISWELL

(B. 1823 POPLAR, LONDON) – BROADMOOR CASE NO. 353

T he 1841 census shows that Sarah was living in Poplar with her younger sisters, Martha, Rose and Mary. By the 1860s, after working her way up through decades of domestic service she had found employment as a lady's maid for the prominent Fuller Maitland family who resided at Remenham Hall in Henley, Berkshire. Ten years later she was living in Hanover Square, Westminster. Both Sarah and her sister Rosina were working as assistant lodging housekeepers for their aunts Isabella and Susannah Potts. Sarah was unmarried, and although she had left the service of the Fuller Maitland family for a seemingly more precarious occupation, she was obviously well-thought of by her previous employers, because, between 1880 and 1883, she was living in the Fullers' Almshouses at Hoxton.

Unfortunately, things then took a turn for the worse for Sarah.

The trial proceedings for the Old Bailey show that Sarah was tried for the attempted murder of her Aunt Isabella on 28 May 1883. The first witness, Mr Croft, in court stated that he was Isabella's neighbour, doing some gardening in his back yard, when Sarah called down to him:

> '"Mr. Croft, will you come in? I have cut my aunt's throat" – I directly went into the house and found the aunt sitting on a chair with a handkerchief to her throat saturated with blood – I asked the prisoner for the razor – she said it was in her pocket; she took it out of her pocket; I took her by the wrist and held her hand till she opened her hand and dropped it – she said "A very dreadful thing this," or something to that effect; "I read

The Old Bailey.

prayers to my aunt this morning and asked her if she was ready to go; she said she was, and I cut her throat".' Sarah appeared calm, and said to the presiding magistrate, 'I did it under the influence that I was going to send her to heaven. she said she thought her aunt would go to glory.' She said she wanted to take her Aunt out of her misery, and to join her dead sister. She then made two sweeping cuts across Isabella's throat.

The witness in the case had known Sarah for a few months, and considered her to be a little disturbed, but not someone who held any animosity towards her aunt, in fact, quite the opposite. She was facing a very long prison sentence for felonious wounding, but the assistant surgeon at Clerkenwell Prison then intervened. He stated to the court that he had been observing the prisoner for over a week. In his medical opinion she was of unsound mind – she had delusions of a religious character – and he considered that Sarah was not responsible for her actions. The judge agreed and announced that Sarah would be 'detained till Her Majesty's pleasure be known'.

Sarah was admitted to Broadmoor on the morning of 2 June 1883. The register and patient files note that she was a

> Single woman, brought from Brentford, no occupation. No epilepsy, believed to be temperate. Church of England. Imperfect education. Indifferent general health, current attack is first, has lasted six weeks. Suicidal and dangerous. Reason for attack: religion. Mother's sister had 'fits'. Father drank and died of consumption. Cause – probably hereditary. Highly excitable. States that she is given over to the Devil and is hopelessly lost. Fancies she sees the Devil. The nurse states that she frequently says she sees spirits and feels she is lost, and that she is deeply despondent and melancholy, and at times much excited.

Two years later we have a glimpse of Sarah's progress at Broadmoor when the authorities replied to a concerned letter. The letter came from Hugh FitzRoy of Morn Lodge, Chickerell:

> She was a faithful servant for many years of my mother's and for some time had one of the family alms-houses, and a more conscilioutous [sic] person I believe never existed.

Dr Orange, the Superintendent replied Sarah

> still continues very melancholic and suicidally disposed. She feels oppressed with a sense of her own utter helplessness and worthlessness and feels she must die. It may be hoped that this distressing state of depression will become ameliorated in course of time.

It seems strange to us today that the letter from a son of a former employer could elicit so much personal information about a patient, but high-born people such as Hugh FitzRoy were treated with an enormous (and incredible) amount of respect by medical authorities in previous times.

Sarah never did fully recover her sanity, and she remained inside Broadmoor for many years. In March 1887 she suffered paralysis while at dinner, and spent time in the Hospital Infirmary. By April she was getting weaker, and her sister Rosina was asked to come to Broadmoor to see her. However, Sarah recovered, and, in fact, it was Rosina who seemed to be in greater need of care. In 1890 Sarah received a letter from her sister Rosina's neighbour, Mrs Ellen Pratt of 147 Bedford Rd, Clapham Park:

> On calling to see your sister yesterday, I found her in a very sad condition both bodily and mentally, I have written to the lawyer stating her cases, she is not fit to look after herself, she does not rest day nor night, but I think if something can be done for her it ought to be done at once without delay. PS – I don't think she ought to have money, she is not fit to be trusted.

Something was done, and Rosina was removed to a county lunatic asylum, and not for the first time as she had previously been admitted to Brookwood Lunatic Asylum, Wandsworth, in 1880. Sarah wrote back to Ellen that she was 'sorry to hear that my dear Sister has had to be put away again, but I know it is the best thing for her. I can only say I am sorry there had to be so much trouble.'

Both sisters were destined to end their days inside institutions. After six years in Broadmoor, Sarah Chiswell died at 12.30 on 24 January 1891 of cerebral haemorrhage in the Hospital Infirmary.

Chapter 24

SARAH JANE DAY

(B. 1828 POPLAR, LONDON) – BROADMOOR NO. 458

In 1882, Sarah Jane Day (described as an elderly woman in the newspapers despite being just 54 years old), was charged with causing the death of her husband, John William Day. Sarah and her husband were both general dealers living in their home town of London. John had not been in the best of health for some time, suffering with both heart and lung disease. Jane, as would soon become very public knowledge, had pronounced problems with alcohol. On one Saturday in June, several of their neighbours saw Jane and John quarrelling in their shop, and they then witnessed Jane picking up a two-pound paperweight from the counter, and strike John three times on the back of the head. He, apparently, was too weak to offer any resistance to the attack. Badly injured by the assault, his health gradually got worse, and he died a few days later. Jane was then charged with manslaughter.

Whilst on remand in Clerkenwell Prison awaiting trial, the Medical Officer diagnosed that, even when her delirium tremens subsided, Sarah still appeared to be suffering from insanity. He ascribed this underlying insanity to the hard drinking she had done for the past two years. Two independent medical experts confirmed she was of unsound mind, and the judge decided that a trial would not be appropriate. Jane was admitted to Broadmoor on 16 June 1882 accompanied by a letter from the Medical Officer:

Dear Sir, the prisoner we send to Broadmoor Criminal Lunatic Asylum has shown symptoms of dementia, was very violent and I had her put in a padded cell ... From enquiries

An alcoholic man with delirium (Wellcome Trust Image L0060780).

I made of her friends, she had been a hard drinker and strange in her mind for almost two years. She labours under strong delusions, is violent at times. She is not subject to fits, is cleanly in her habits, and is taking her food well.

Broadmoor agreed with this assessment, noting that Sarah was,

dangerous to others. Strange delusions. Thinks she is poisoned that they are going to boil her down or that she is going to be killed. Sees people walking up and down in front of her. Hears people talking to her outside the prison. Appears to have shown indications of insanity for a year or two before she committed the offence and to have been at the time suffering from delirium tremens from excessive drinking. No history of insanity, intemperance or consumption among her relatives. Cause; intemperance in drink.

During her lifetime, Sarah had borne nine children, only four of whom were still alive when she entered Broadmoor. Her bereavement of five children may very well have contributed to her problematic drinking in the first place. Her family remained sympathetic to Sarah throughout her incarceration. It was one of her daughters who first petitioned for Sarah to be released early into their care. Her married daughter and her husband, Mr and Mrs Clark, offered to look after her in their home in Rotherhithe in 1884. The Superintendent, Dr Orange, considered that it was not safe to release Sarah at that time. They tried again in 1886 when Mr Clark petitioned for release on the grounds that his mother-in-law was now 'quite rational'. The Broadmoor authorities continued to be sceptical: 'this woman is going on satisfactorily; but her mental condition is not such as would make it advisable for her to be set at large'. James Clark was persistent, and applied again in 1888, and again in 1890. This last time with success.

The Medical Report that Broadmoor made out on Sarah at that point stated:

She has shown no indications of insanity for several years. She is of a harmless disposition and is industrious in her habits her daughter and son in law are quite able and anxious to give her a home and to look carefully after her and to report if she relapses into habits of intemperance or shows signs again or becoming insane. She will not be benefited by her detention being prolonged. Under all the circumstances I think she might, without unwarrantable risk, be permitted to go to the care of her daughter . . .

Jane was then discharged to the home of James and Eliza Clark at 334 Rotherhithe Street, London on 14 October 1890.

In January 1891 Broadmoor sent a questionnaire to Sarah's daughter, which she was required to get signed by a local priest, to testify that her mother was still safe to be at large and not intemperate. We do not have the questionnaire, or the comments made by the priest, but in March 1891 two of Broadmoor's attendants were dispatched to the Clarks' house to bring Sarah back to the hospital. Sarah was taken back into custody and her conditional licence was revoked following her 'relapse', as Broadmoor termed it. Following a bout of influenza Sarah then contracted pneumonia. She died on 10 April 1891.

Sarah had spent nearly ten years inside Broadmoor suffering from a form of mental illness, brought about, at least in part, by her heavy drinking. It may seem harsh that someone who was clearly mentally ill and suffering from alcoholism was locked away from society rather than being treated in an open hospital, but it must be remembered that capital punishment still existed for murder at this time. At the cost of spending the last decade of her life inside a secure hospital, Sarah had escaped the gallows, or at least many hard years in a convict prison.

Chapter 25

SARAH TUFF ALIAS SARAH POOLE

(B. 1841 BRISTOL) – CONVICT H.202

S usan Poole, a butcher's daughter, was born in Bristol in 1841. She was only 17 when she was first convicted of larceny, but the newspaper already noted that she was a 'girl of loose character, co-habiting with a thief', and living in a 'nest of thieves'. Her second conviction followed in 1859, when she was found guilty at Bristol magistrates' court for uttering counterfeit coin (trying to pass the bad coins off in a shop). She received an eight-month sentence on top of the four months she had already served in a local prison. She would next experience the rigours of the convict system when she was convicted of an indictable offence. On 16 April 1863, Sarah was convicted of larceny from the person (stealing a purse) at Bristol Quarter Sessions. Because she already had previous convictions she received three years' penal servitude. The local newspaper described her as 'a diminutive, repulsive looking woman'.

She served two and a half years in prison and was then released on a conditional licence (a ticket-of-leave). It was not long before she was remanded back into custody accused of stealing a ring and some money from a married man. Again, the newspaper described Sarah in derogatory terms, 'an old offender on a ticket of leave', but the presiding magistrate was, surprisingly, just as critical of her victim, suggesting that men who used prostitutes should expect to be victims of theft. The case never came to trial.

In September 1866 Sarah married George Tuff. Far from this providing stability, five years after standing side-by-side in a Bristol church, they stood side-by-side in the dock, accused of larceny. The case against her husband was dismissed, but she received four months. Her previous convictions had weighed heavily against her. This was the last time George would ever appear in court, but Sarah was back in court, and back in prison, in 1875. Convicted of shoplifting at Bristol Sessions she then served another year, followed by three years' police supervision. It did not take very long before she was in trouble again. In 1876 she was convicted of larceny at Bristol Sessions. The judges imposed seven years' penal servitude in a convict prison sentence and five years' police supervision.

Sarah's prison record was updated every time she moved into a different prison. As with all convicts, Sarah spent the first nine months in a silent system where she was kept from all the other prisoners. She then served time in Fulham, Bristol, Millbank (again) and Woking Female Prison. She was recorded as having an imperfect education, a broken nose, her left ear torn, scars on lips and forehead, and pierced ears. She also had syphilis. This may explain why her nose was disfigured and she had lost her four front teeth.

In 1879, Sarah received a letter from her sister-in-law, a long-standing brothel-keeper who had served time herself in the past for several felonies. It appeared that Sarah's husband, a large wagon driver, no longer wanted Sarah to return to the marital home. After spending some time in Russell House Refuge in Streatham, London, she was released on conditional licence with three years of her sentence not served. Without a home to return to, she may have stayed with her sister-in-law or gone to another friend, or maybe she slept out on the streets. We do know that she returned to Bristol as, after three weeks of freedom, she was back at Bristol Quarter Sessions.

Convicted of stealing boots and a basket after four previous convictions for larceny, she was sentenced to five years' penal servitude, followed by two years' police supervision. On this sentence, she was punished for talking during solitary exercise, and loudly complaining when she was told to be quiet, for quarrelling with another prisoner, for breaking her toilet pan, and for throwing down her stool in a temper. This may have been a factor in her petition to be

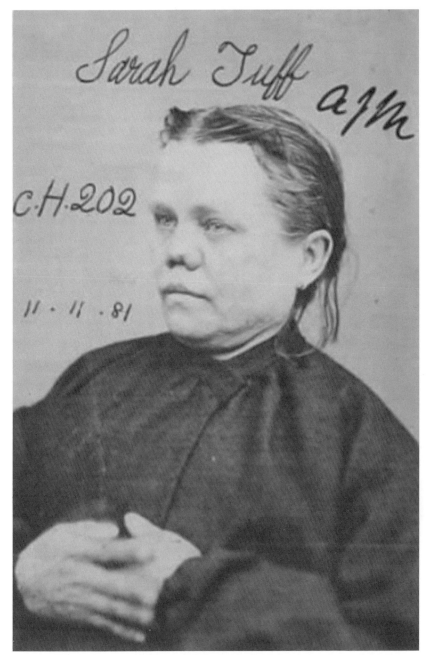

Sarah Tuff. Courtesy of TNA, PCOM4; Piece: 66; Item: 3

released early on health grounds (syphilis) being rejected in February 1885. In September, she repetitioned again, this time promising good behaviour in the future. The Home Secretary told the Governor of Woking Female Prison that she would 'be considered for release on license when she has completed another year – to be told that her conduct in prison will be monitored until then'. With no more prison indiscipline in the next twelve months, she was granted conditional early release by the Home Secretary in March 1886. After release, she returned to Bristol. She did not commit any further crimes, possibly she had reformed, or possibly she was too ill, and in need of care, to offend. There was no free medical care in this period, and the only support the state offered came in the form of the workhouse. In 1891 she was living in Barton Regis Workhouse, Winterbourne, in Gloucester. She was a 60-year-old woman with advanced syphilis, and a long offending record. Aged 65, she died in the institution.

Chapter 26

SUSANNAH WELLS ALIAS WATSON

(B. 1819 WEDGEBURY) – CONVICT 885

Susannah Wells was employed as a pastry cook by some of the most well-known men in England. She had worked for the Earl of Derby, three times Prime Minister, for six years, and for Sir Joshua Jebb for three years. At the time she was cooking tasty pastries for Jebb, he was Governor of Pentonville Prison. She may well have still been working for him when she was convicted of fraud at Middlesex Sessions on 17 September 1847. There are no details of the case recorded in the Criminal Registers, except that she received three months' custody for the offence, but we may assume that she was found stealing from her master, since this was also the offence she was charged with three years later.

In 1850, aged 30, Susannah stood in the dock of the Old Bailey accused of stealing a gold chain, a watch and several other items from her master's shop in London. In May 1850 *The Standard* revealed that, when examined by the magistrate at Mansion House, she confessed that she had sold on the watch to a jeweller in Seven Dials, London. Found guilty, the judges had a range of sentences available to them. Her former employer, Sir Joshua Jebb, had been made Chair of the Board of Directors of Convict Prisons that same year, and Susannah could well have ended up in one of his prisons. However, the judges decided that Susannah would be sent to the Australian penal colonies instead, and she was sentenced to be 'transported beyond the seas' for a period of seven years.

The convict ship Success *docked at Hobart.*

She sailed on the convict transport ship *Emma Eugenia* arriving at Van Diemen's Land on 7 March 1851. She was described in the Tasmanian convict records as a 5 foot tall, 30-year-old woman, with a sallow complexion, brown hair and blue eyes, with a large mole on her left cheek. The convict authorities kept details of each convict's appearance, their past crimes – which were self-confessed by each convict – and their behaviour whilst under sentence. Male convicts served part of their sentences as assigned agricultural labour to free settlers, or in gangs assigned to public works clearing bush and building roads. Female convicts were kept in the Female

Penitentiary, worked in the Female Factory, or were assigned as domestic workers to free settlers. Susannah was assigned to a farm outside of Hobart, and frequently breached convict regulations. On 26 September 1851 she was Absent Without Leave and sentenced to hard labour as a punishment; on 23 April 1852 she was found to be drunk on her master's premises and sentenced to four months' hard labour. Six months later she was Absent Without Leave again, and this time she received nine months' hard labour. The following year she married fellow convict William Watson. In 1855, she was Absent Without Leave again, and she was punished with another month of hard labour. That was the last time she was in trouble whilst under sentence.

Susannah received a ticket-of-leave, and conditional release in 1856. So long as convicts complied with the conditions of their licence (which could be obeying a curfew, keeping away from certain geographical areas, not reoffending and so on) and carried their ticket to show to a constable if required, they would then be deemed to be free. Because Susannah had been sentenced to seven years' transportation she was then free to leave the colony if she wished. Any convict who had received a life sentence was barred from returning to Britain.

There are no reports of anyone called either Susannah Wells or Susannah Watson being before the Tasmanian courts after 1853. Perhaps married life settled Susannah down, or she decided to reform her ways, or perhaps the couple escaped Hobart as soon as they could, and sailed for Melbourne. Gold had been discovered in the colony of Victoria in 1851 and many convicts left Tasmania as soon as they could to try and find the fortune. Susannah had once had an eye for gold, so the opportunities provided by the Victorian goldfields may well have appealed to her and her new husband.

Chapter 27

AMELIA LAYTON

(B. C.1840 LONDON) – THIRTY YEARS OF INSTITUTIONALISATION

Despite the fact that the movement in and out of different institutions over a lifetime created a long and deep documentary trail for some women, it can still be virtually impossible to know where they came from. Amelia Layton is one such case. Amelia was born in Middlesex in the late 1830s. It is not possible to know exactly when, as, at various points in her life, Amelia's date of birth was reported as anywhere from 1833 to 1844. For most of her life, Amelia reported herself as a widow, but there is little evidence to show that she was ever married. The first records that can be attributed to our Amelia, and not one of the three other women of the same name and age as her living in London, was in 1868, when Amelia would have been around the age of 30. We know that, at that time, Amelia was admitted to the Strand Union Workhouse for two days in early November, before being discharged at her own request.

It was not unusual for individuals to resort to the workhouse in times of difficulty. This was particularly true of women, who were more vulnerable than men to personal and financial crisis (such as poor employment prospects, the loss of a family breadwinner, pre- or extra-marital pregnancy, and so on). Women like Amelia might submit themselves, as a temporary measure, to the discipline of the workhouse when funds were sparse or lodgings difficult to come by. It certainly seems like the late 1860s were uncertain times for Amelia, who returned to the workhouse again a few months later in January 1869.

Amelia Layton. Courtesy of TNA, MEPO6/80 Prisoner 393b

However, Amelia managed to stay clear of state institutions for almost the next decade, finding enough work as an artificial flower-maker to get by. It wasn't until the summer of 1877 that Amelia returned to the workhouse, for two weeks, again being discharged at her own request in August. Amelia returned twice to the workhouse that same month, and then again in December. She returned yet another time in February 1878. Amelia's use of the workhouse was still episodic, suggesting she was again dealing with some kind of temporary crisis. Although, unlike her first admission in the 1860s, this time the crisis seemed to last for longer, or Amelia lacked the capacity to deal with it quickly. Amelia returned to the workhouse again the following year in 1879 for a brief stay. The poverty Amelia seemed to be experiencing became more chronic than acute, and in 1881, as she sought a new way to deal with her financial problems, she turned to the dubious solution of theft. Amelia was indicted on three separate charges for stealing blankets from Mary Elsey, a pair of sheets from Sarah Vincent and a looking glass from Morris Cohen. For her trouble she was sentenced to twelve months in prison.

Spending some time in prison appears to have dissuaded Amelia from reoffending, and perhaps also put her off seeking help from other state institutions. Amelia did not return to the workhouse for almost a decade. Instead she continued to ply her trade as a flower-maker, living in a series of casual lodging houses, and unfortunately, she then turned to drink. In September 1890 she was summoned to appear before a magistrate for drunkenness but she failed to come to court, sinking instead into the shadows of the city.

Amelia's life again began to spiral beyond her control. In January 1892 she returned to the workhouse for help, only to be discharged. In April 1892 her drinking saw her committed to Hanwell County Lunatic Asylum for a month, before she was discharged from there too. The following year she returned to the workhouse, but was only allowed to stay for two days before she was turned out. She returned again a few months later and stayed for a little over a week before being discharged again. She was back less than a month later. For the authorities, Amelia was no longer a respectable woman experiencing crisis, but an indigent burden, to be addressed and dismissed as quickly as possible.

Amelia approached the workhouse again for help in March 1894, but was turned away. That same day Amelia made a very public attempt at suicide. She walked into a Clerkenwell pub and asked for a glass of water into which she poured some 'white precipitate powder'. Amelia then proceeded to drink the mixture in front of a crowd and claim 'I have taken poison', which was later confirmed by a doctor. Amelia was given over to police custody at which point she exclaimed 'I want to die; I've had a lot of trouble'. She was remanded in custody but ultimately discharged by the sitting magistrate. Amelia returned to the workhouse where she stayed for almost two weeks before asking to be discharged. Amelia was clearly seeking some kind of help, for her poverty, her personal circumstances or her addiction, but failing to find it.

The following year Amelia was charged at Clerkenwell Police Court with being drunk and incapable, but once again she failed to turn up at court for her trial. A few months later she returned to the workhouse, and readmitted herself again and again – a total of three times in 1896. Amelia stayed out of trouble for almost a year, but by 1898, thirty years after her first admission, she was back to admitting herself to the workhouse on an almost monthly basis. Regular institutionalisation followed, and Amelia spent census night of 1901 at the workhouse. A few months later when she was again 'at large', the following newspaper report appeared:

TRYING TO DRINK HERSELF TO DEATH:

A Middle aged Widow named Amelia Leyton living at St John's Wood-Terrace, was charged on remand with being drunk and incapable of taking care of herself at Adelaide-road – Interrogated by the magistrate the prisoner said; 'I shall drink myself to death. I am trying to do it as much as ever I can, though I am sorry to say so.' – She was remanded that the state of her mind might be enquired into and it was now reported that she had shown no indications of insanity and the magistrate told her to go away and keep sober.

Unfortunately, the solution to Amelia's problems was not nearly so simple. She returned to the workhouse in August the following year, and stayed for almost four months until the beginning of 1903. The following year, after another stay in the workhouse, it was finally recognised that the current systems of court, imprisonment and the workhouse were failing to deal adequately with Amelia.

On 13 October 1904, Amelia was convicted of drunk and disorderly conduct at Marlborough Street police court. This time, an exasperated magistrate ordered Amelia to be taken to a reformatory for criminal inebriates–a secure institution, halfway between prison and hospital, in which those designated as habitual drunkards could be detained for longer periods of time than standard terms of imprisonment for drunkenness allowed. At the inebriates home, Amelia was one of almost two hundred women kept to a strict routine of chores, healthy living and sobriety. Amelia was committed to the reformatory for two years. She was released in October 1906, but in less than two months had relapsed into old habits. She was brought to the dock at Bow Street Police court, and ordered back to the reformatory for another three years.

Amelia's case was unusual. Given that space at inebriate homes was far outweighed by the number of habitual drunkards plaguing the courts, magistrates usually only gave offenders one chance to make it through the reformatory system. If they failed to maintain sobriety, they would not normally be offered a second chance of help. Amelia though, perhaps due to advanced age (she was now in her late sixties and one of the oldest women in the reformatory), was felt to merit another opportunity. Another three years at the home did little to encourage reform in Amelia, however. When she was released in 1909, she arrived almost immediately at the workhouse, and resumed the familiar cycle of admission, discharge and problematic drinking. She was sentenced a third time to an inebriate reformatory in 1910, and remained there, in Lancashire, until 1913, when she made her way back to London.

The end of Amelia's story was not a happy one. Although there are no more records of convictions for drunkenness, Amelia returned to the workhouse a year after arriving home. She died there in 1915, estimated to be approximately 80 years old.

Chapter 28

ANN PLOWMAN

(B. 1866 TAUNTON) – HABITUAL OFFENDER

L ife for many working women in this period was precarious. For those at the bottom of the social and economic spectrum, existence was a balancing act, in which relationships, employment, money and respectability all had to be tightly managed, for if any one element spiralled out of control, the rest might also unravel with alarming speed.

Ann Yard was born in Taunton, Somerset, in 1866. She was one of thousands of children whose start in life may have heavily influenced the direction of her adult life. Born to Thomas, an agricultural labourer, and Elizabeth, a glove maker, both Somerset locals, the family were severely impoverished, and by the time she was 13, Ann was living with her parents and seven younger siblings in the Taunton Union Workhouse.

As with many poor young women keen to escape the poverty of youth and establish their own homes, Ann married as soon as she was able to. When she was 21, she married William Alfred Plowman, a labourer who over the next two decades of their life together, would earn a living at a variety of low-skilled manual jobs from farm work to chimney sweeping. Even without the six children they would have together in the next decade, the Plowman couple almost immediately found themselves struggling for money. William's work as a chimney sweep, porter and casual labourer brought in no more than 5s. a day. With five children under the age of 10 to provide for by the 1890s, Ann too had to go out to work. As their financial situation worsened, Ann took increasingly precarious employment which earned scant funds for the family, and began a chain of events that led the family to disaster.

Poverty in Victorian Britain.

The nature of Ann's employment was never made explicitly clear in records, but information included in newspaper reports suggests that Ann undertook various activities, from charring (doing housework for money) and laundry, to street selling. Work on the streets was not only low paid, but also often brought women to the attention of the police.

Ann's first brush with the law came in 1898 when she narrowly avoided a night in the local lock-up for being drunk and disorderly. Instead, she was fined one shilling. With court costs of 5d. this was a fair sum for the Plowmans to find. Ann's housekeeping money from William was just 5s. a week. A year later in 1899, Ann was back in court charged with using obscene language in the street. A police constable testified to seeing Ann in the company of two soldiers and a group of other women one night in September. The inference was that the women were working as prostitutes. The soldiers were moved on by the constable, and in her frustration at the constable for causing her to lose trade, Ann reportedly 'turned round on him and abused him in the most obscene manner'. For this crime, Ann was fined 10s. and 7s. for the cost of the court case. The total cost to the Plowmans was three days of William's wages, a sum they could scarce afford. Ann had to spend increasing amounts of time out of the home searching for work.

Ann found herself back in court a few months later, in December 1899, but this time she was not a defendant, but a witness at the Coroner's Court. Ann's daughter, Hilda Jane, had burnt to death at the family's home one morning in early November. Like many women juggling the need to work and family responsibilities, Ann's children were often left unattended. On the days when she sought work, and her eldest son Joseph (aged 9) was out working with his father, her eldest daughter Hilda Jane (age 6) was left in sole charge of her younger siblings. Ann left the house at around 9.30am one morning, leaving Hilda responsible for looking after her siblings. The Victorian home could be a dangerous place, and in mid-winter, it had taken less than an hour for Hilda to come into contact with the flames of the open fire. She sustained severe burns to her left arm, body and face. Despite being rescued by a neighbour and taken almost immediately to hospital, Hilda died from her injuries a month later. The judge did not seek to prosecute the Plowmans for negligence, as it was legal for children to be left at home unattended, though he chastised both William and Ann – William for not having the money to allow his wife not to work, and Ann not for finding a more suitable minder for her young children.

It is hard to imagine the extent to which the loss of their daughter in such tragic circumstances affected the Plowmans. What we do know is that William and Ann separated in around 1906, and Ann began living on her own. In future Ann referred to herself intermittently as married or widowed. Ann and William do not appear to have ever reconciled. William moved elsewhere in Somerset and died in 1934. Shortly after the breakdown of their parents' marriage, Ann's remaining children under the age of 16, Blanche, Olive and John, were sent to the Home of the Good Shepherd Industrial School in Leytonstone, London. They would never see their mother again. Ann's eldest son, Joseph, joined the military. There are no records for him after the First World War.

Now without the support and relative stability of her family, or the incentive of her children to keep Ann living within the confines of the law, Ann's drunkenness and disorderly behaviour began to garner significantly more attention. In 1906 Ann was arrested for being drunk in a pub, refusing to leave when ordered, and breaking a pane of glass at the Parade Hotel. Although Ann claimed to be a teetotaller (after suffering from an illness), several witnesses attested to her wandering around the streets in a state of drunkenness. The fines for the offence amounted to almost 25s. She couldn't pay that sort of sum. In default of payment, Ann was sent to prison for three weeks.

Around this time, Ann began a relationship with James 'Jimmy' Dodden. The pair began lodging together in Alfred Street, Taunton. James had his own long string of previous convictions for violence and drunkenness stretching back to childhood, and both he and Ann continued to be in and out of court. While Ann and Jimmy may have been acquainted for some time, having spent years living in the same community, their new relationship was volatile and intensified Ann's troubles.

In 1907, Ann was again given heavy fines and a term of imprisonment in lieu of payment when she entered the Parade Hotel (from which she had been barred) looking for Jimmy. When she found him there drinking but she herself was refused service, she became agitated and picked up a mug and a glass and threw them at the landlord. A month later Ann was back in court after a public row on the street at night with Jimmy. She was prosecuted for drunk and disorderly behaviour. At the same session, Ann attempted to prosecute Jimmy for assault, alleging that on the same night, after leaving another pub together, Jimmy abused her on the street and 'knocked her down three times'. Both Ann and Jimmy were bound over for twelve months to keep the peace, and Ann was fined another 5s. for drunk and disorderly conduct.

Ann's good behaviour lasted less than six months before she was back in court in January 1908 charged with another assault. Having barged into a lodging house looking for Jimmy, Ann had assaulted Elizabeth Widger, knocking her down, pulling her hair, kicking her and striking her face. Ann also faced a second separate charge of drunk and disorderly conduct. She was given one month of hard labour. After her release from prison, Ann continued to harass Elizabeth Widger, threatening her in the street on several occasions. Ann was given another fine, and required to provide £5 sureties of her good behaviour for six months. Unable to pay either, she was sent to Exeter Gaol for a week.

Ann was back in court the following year, 1909, and the papers noted that she 'occasionally relieves the possible monotony of her existence by breaking out in a sort of frenzied manner. At such times she seems to let herself go completely, and the sequel is invariably at the police court.' On this occasion, there were four charges against her: one for drunk and disorderly behaviour at the Half Moon Inn, to which she pleaded guilty, two for criminal damage to glasses, and an assault on Clara Allen, the daughter of the landlord. Ann spent another two and a half months in prison.

The more convictions Ann received, the more notorious she became with the police, courts, pubs and with the local community. It became difficult for Ann to leave the house without finding herself in some kind of altercation. In 1910, Ann was prosecuted for throwing stones and breaking windows at a house in which she suspected Jimmy Dodden was hiding, and with drunk and disorderly behaviour. A few months later she was back in court again charged with an assault on Amelia Cox. When Amelia entered the pub in which Ann was drinking, looking for her husband, she made the mistake of asking Jimmy Dodden if he had seen him. A jealous Ann threw a glass at Amelia's face. She was also charged with drunk and disorderly conduct in refusing to leave the pub. The magistrate believed Ann's explanation that the glass had been meant for Jimmy and not Amelia, but she was fined 20s. and costs all the same.

Throughout this time Ann was still earning a living as a prostitute. In September of 1910, she was convicted of stealing a silver watch and chain from one of her customers. By the time she appeared at the October sessions, she had nineteen previous offences recorded against her, for drunkenness, obscenity, damage and assault. Ann and Jimmy continued living together on the proceeds of Ann's prostitution, a cause of considerable antagonism between them. In 1911 Ann was charged with drunk and disorderly behaviour, trying to kick down the door of a pub in which Jimmy was drinking, exclaiming loudly that he was inside drinking her money. She was sent to prison for a month. Upon her release, she was almost immediately apprehended by the police for behaving like a 'wild woman' staggering in the street using obscene and abusive language. In the following months Ann was in and out of court, testifying to magistrates that she 'would rather go to prison than to a home', a wish possibly stemming from her earliest experiences as a child in the workhouse; that request was invariably granted.

In the years leading up to the First World War, Ann was charged with more counts of drunkenness, prostitution and theft, spending many months in prison. She has more than forty appearances in court recorded against her. Ann's convictions continued throughout wartime as she proceeded to solicit for prostitution with soldiers, and drink heavily. Ann was suspected to be suffering from syphilis by this time, and in 1916 a magistrate noted 'no doubt the defendant was a source of great danger to soldiers, and she would have to go to prison for three months with hard labour'.

Ann's mode of life continued until the end of the war, at which point her appearances in court abruptly stopped when she was moved to a charitable home for the elderly and destitute (where she died in 1922). While there were undoubtedly several interlinking factors which contributed to Ann's long offending career, the intense poverty of her early life was key to the downward spiral which saw a young married mother of six see her marriage break down, her children taken from her, her opportunities for work shrink and her problem with alcohol deepen.

Chapter 29

ELIZABETH COPPIN

(B. 1853 MAIDSTONE) – MULTIPLE INSTITUTIONS

Elizabeth Coppin was born in Maidstone, Kent, in 1853. Her father, John, was a local man himself who worked as a labourer. Her mother, Ann, was originally from Ireland and may well have been one of the thousands that arrived in England as refugees from the Great Famine. Elizabeth was the eldest of three siblings, having two younger brothers: John two years younger than her, and William, seven years her junior.

At the age of just 11, Elizabeth was placed in the dock of Maidstone Police court, charged with stealing three neck scarves. One she sold on; the others she took home with her which her mother discovered. Elizabeth was identified as the culprit of the theft by some of the multiple witnesses that were gathered around the doorway to the shop from which the scarves were taken. She was apprehended and brought before the magistrates. Elizabeth was described in court as 'the eldest of three orphans' despite her mother being present in court. This might suggest that by this time her father, the family breadwinner, had died. Elizabeth certainly received the sympathy of the court, either because of her youth, or the family's circumstances. Elizabeth had not been convicted previously, and because of her former good character, the magistrate discharged her with only a reprimand.

Unfortunately, whatever circumstances led to Elizabeth's first offence were not as easily dealt with. Just three weeks after she was discharged, Elizabeth again found herself in the dock at Maidstone Police Court. On this occasion, Elizabeth was charged with having stolen a plum cake from a local shop. Though she was still just

Westmorland Lock Hospital, Dublin, 1899.

11 years old, Elizabeth's previous conviction for the scarves was taken as evidence of her incorrigible character. Elizabeth faced the full brunt of the adult law, and she was sentenced to one month of hard labour in an adult prison, followed by four years in a juvenile reformatory.

By the time Elizabeth was released from the reformatory at the age of 16 in 1869, not only was her father dead but her family had disbanded. Elizabeth did not return home to her mother, Ann, who perhaps destitute, remarried, relocated or dead, disappeared from formal records. Elizabeth's younger brothers had both been placed in the Union Workhouse School in a small suburb of Maidstone. At the age of 16, Elizabeth found herself liberated, but alone.

Though reformatories often took great care in training girls in their care to be fit for employment on release – domestic skills were thought key in helping women maintain moral, productive, law-abiding lives – Elizabeth would have found it hard to establish herself in a stable life upon release. Demand for good employment positions outstripped the supply of poor working women looking for them. Those whose reputation had been tarnished by conviction or incarceration often found it difficult to obtain decent work or lodgings in any case. On top of the standard difficulties faced by women in her position, Elizabeth was released at a time when policing and the law had shifted to place many ex-offenders like her in an even more precarious position.

Habitual offender legislation passed at the end of the 1860s gave police the power to surveil, apprehend and prosecute known 'habitual offenders' (anyone convicted of more than two offences) suspected of planning further wrongdoing; and the advent of the Contagious Diseases Acts in 1866, 1868 and 1869 legislated for the apprehension and detention of women suspected of working as common prostitutes in eighteen districts in England and Ireland, and a ten mile radius around these areas, one of which was Chatham in Kent.

After her release from the reformatory, with limited opportunities for employment, 16-year-old Elizabeth may well have turned to prostitution as a method of subsistence. She must, at some point in 1870 or 1871, have been arrested by police in Chatham as a prostitute, as by early 1871 she was confined in the Chatham Lock Hospital, a small institution housing almost fifty women between the ages of 16 and 32 who had been apprehended as 'common prostitutes' and found to be suffering from a sexually transmitted infection. Elizabeth would have spent between three months and one year in the lock hospital before release, during which time she would have been required to undergo mandatory treatments, including hot and cold baths, the application of mercury to infected sores or internal injections. When appraised by medical staff to be 'cured' (although venereal disease remained incurable until the discovery of penicillin half a century later), Elizabeth would have been released with a certificate of clean health, and she could have then continued to work as a prostitute.

Prostitution is one of the hardest offences to trace for women. While some were prosecuted in the courts, only a small proportion of the thousands of prostitutes in nineteenth-century England were ever imprisoned for the trade. Often it is impossible to tell whether women arrested as prostitutes, for drunkenness, disorder and public obscenity, truly were sex-workers, or were simply disorderly women in public spaces.

It is not possible to ascertain whether Elizabeth did return to work as a prostitute after her release. However, we do know that over the next decade, Elizabeth continued to live on the margins of society. Though there are no records of criminal conviction or imprisonment for her, she may well have continued to work as a prostitute, or perhaps she made a living through a range of informal and undocumented employments like charring (cleaning), hawking (street-selling), sweated labour or taking in laundry. By 1881 Elizabeth was living as a lodger at number 7 Seaton Court, in Upton, on the outskirts of London. She was working as a laundress and sharing her accommodation with fifteen strangers.

Elizabeth never married or established a stable home for herself. Like many women who had been in and out of penal institutions since childhood, and who battled with lifelong poverty, Eliza found it difficult to recover. With a damaged reputation from her time working as a prostitute, both personal relationships and steady employment would have been hard to find. Elizabeth died at the age of 46. Although a relatively young age, this is perhaps not surprising given that she may have been suffering with syphilis for up to thirty years.

Chapter 30

ELLEN RISDEN

(B. 1842 CO. CORK) – CONVICT

Ellen Mahoney was born in Cork, Ireland, in 1842, just a few years before the Irish famine devastated the country. Those from the south and west of Ireland experienced some of the worst privations. Many families flocked from the rural lands of Ireland to the cities in search of help, only to find their best hope for survival was emigration. Ellen was one of thousands of children who travelled with families that could not afford tickets to Australia, Canada or America, who found themselves deposited in England's port towns and cities, starving and impoverished.

Boats carrying refugees from Cork and Waterford commonly landed in Bristol, and while for some it was only a temporary stay before a journey onwards, for the Mahoney family, Bristol became their new home. Managing to navigate the immediate trauma and poverty caused by emigration, the Mahoneys settled in the city. Local populations could be hostile to Irish settlers, however, and policing practices often targeted Irish settled areas as particular sites of drunkenness, disorder and violence. The Mahoneys were a relatively law-abiding family, but as Ellen reached her late teens, she found herself in court on a couple of occasions charged with drunkenness.

At the age of 18, in 1860, Ellen married Edward Risden, a railway porter almost ten years her senior. In the following decade the pair had five children. Yet all was not well in the Risden household. In 1866, less than a year after the birth of their daughter Ann, Edward Risden took out a notice in the local paper, stating:

Ellen Risden. Courtesy of TNA, PCOM4; Piece: 48; Item: 13.

I hearby give notice that I will not be answerable for any debt or debts that my wife Ellen Risden may contract in my name after this date.

While the exact circumstances that led Edward to take out the notice are not clear (other than Ellen running up large debts that he was clearly unhappy about paying!) the couple continued living together, and had a further two children in the next two years. Although she did not run up any more debts, Ellen's disorderly behaviour continued. In 1868 Ellen was taken to court and fined 2s. for an assault on Catherine Cater, a neighbour. A few years later, although still living with and supported by Edward, Ellen began to steal. This was perhaps a tactic to acquire the goods or raise the money that Edward's notice had temporarily denied her. In 1873, Ellen stole a pair of boots and was given one month in prison with hard labour, the following year she again stole boots and received two months of hard labour. Ellen's offences were infrequent, rather than perpetual, taking place less than once a year. This would suggest that her thefts were not closely related to financial hardship or destitution. Ellen offended again in 1874, 1876 and 1879, receiving two, four and six months of hard labour respectively. It does not seem likely that Edward and Ellen were living together during this time.

In 1880, Ellen's luck changed. After stealing a shawl, she was sentenced to five years in convict prison, and three years' police supervision following that. Ellen was a well-behaved prisoner, but while she was serving time in Millbank Prison, the staff wrote to Edward to inform him his wife was pregnant. Ellen gave birth to the baby, a boy, John, in Westminster Prison, and after she was allowed to nurse him almost a year, the child was transferred to a London workhouse alone while Ellen finished her sentence. The boy was given Risden's surname, but never claimed by Edward, who continued to care for their other children. He may well not have been Edward's biological son.

After her release from prison in 1883, Ellen went straight back to Bristol, and straight back to offending. Her lifestyle was evidently beginning to impact more heavily on those around her. A few months after her release, in February 1884, Ellen was charged with stealing a chemise from her daughter Ann and 'feloniously pawning' it. Ann saw the shawl in the pawnshop and begged her father to redeem it, although Edward claimed he had not the means to do so. Ann, rather unwillingly, asked the police to intervene, although a magistrate later dismissed the case as just a family squabble. Ann claimed that her mother 'sold everything for drink', a charge which Ellen denied.

In 1886 Ellen was again in court for theft, charged with stealing 20 yards of flannel. She called her youngest daughter to act as a witness for her defence, but instead the girl gave conflicting evidence, and actually helped to convict her mother. Ellen was sent to prison for three months, much to the relief of her family.

Ellen was convicted of stealing boots again in 1889, and spent another nine months in prison after an 1890 conviction for larceny. As Ellen entered her fifties, her quality of life deteriorated, and she began to steal for subsistence. In 1894, she was convicted of stealing bread and butter, and given twelve months in prison. After release in 1895, Ellen managed to desist from crime (or at least evade detection) for almost three years, until she was back to stealing boots, convicted twice for this in 1898. At this point in her life, Ellen had been in and out of prison almost constantly for thirty years, and had a criminal record that spanned forty years, almost two-thirds of her life.

After release from prison, Ellen had little other option but to turn to the workhouse. Unfortunately, her violent temper ensured that she did not stay there for long. In July 1899 Ellen was charged with breaking three panes of glass and a basin in the Union Workhouse. She complained of bad treatment at the hands of the Guardians and stated she would 'sooner be in Exeter Gaol than in the workhouse'. Her wish was granted, and she was sent to prison for fourteen days. Upon release, she immediately stole a coat and was sent back to prison again. After release, unable to return to her family and unwilling to return to the workhouse, Ellen entered the Bristol District Refuge for Penitent Women, a special home for ex-offenders attempting to turn their lives around. She spent two years in the institution before she left of her own accord and returned to offending. Ellen was imprisoned again in 1904 and 1905 for the theft of boots.

Now in her sixties, with more than a dozen offences behind her, known to the police and courts as a habitual offender and her age making other employment unlikely, Ellen had no other way to subsist than to rely on institutions or to turn to theft. It was often very difficult for those that had spent decades of their lives living transient and chaotic lives to exist peacefully within the strict regimes of voluntary institutions like inebriate or penitent homes, or within the disciplined world of the workhouse, and for many, theft and freedom (even with the constant risk of imprisonment) were preferable to living under such tight moral and physical constraints.

However, life on the streets was hard, and the older and more infirm an offender became, the harder it got to survive. Despite her resistance to institutions throughout her life, by the age of 69, Ellen had nowhere else to turn to but the workhouse. She remained a resident in a local workhouse until her death in 1915 at the age of 73. Ellen never, in all her years of testimony and incarceration, offered an explanation as to why she rejected her home and family for a life of habitual offending instead.

Chapter 31

MARIA DIBSDALE

(B. 1866 NEWPORT, WALES) – HABITUAL DRUNK

A large number of court cases involving female defendants were for drunkenness, and many women were in court multiple times accused of being 'in their cups'. However, rather than all women conforming to the stereotype of the habitual drunk roaming the streets, and finding themselves in prison on a regular basis for disturbing public order, some women who found themselves at odds with the law due to drink were indistinguishable from their respectable friends and neighbours living in the leafy suburbs of England.

Maria Lloyd was born in Newport, south Wales, in 1866, the daughter of Daniel Lloyd, a railway engine driver, and his wife Emma. Engine drivers were considered to be part of the 'labour aristocracy' and the Lloyds were a respectable working-class family. Maria had an older brother, Richard, who joined their father working on the railway, and two younger brothers also. Maria, unlike many of her peers, attended school until the relatively late age of 14.

At 18, Maria travelled to London to seek work as a domestic servant. Within two years, she had met and married Charles Dibsdale, a postman. In their first year of marriage, a daughter was born to the pair, and two years later, a second child was born. In the decade that followed their marriage, Charles and Maria had a total of eight children together, though only five (their two daughters and three sons) survived infancy.

The family settled in North London, and appear to have had a relatively stable life together. Charles's job provided enough money to live fairly comfortably, leaving Maria at home to look after the

Maria Dibsdale. Courtesy of TNA, MEPO6/78 Prisoner 394.

children. For many families this arrangement may have been preferable to juggling childcare and gruelling paid employment. For other women, however, a life that revolved solely around their house and children could be empty, isolating and tedious. In such circumstances, many otherwise ordinary housewives turned to the destructive habit of drink.

We cannot be certain when Maria began drinking, but drink she did. By the first few years of the twentieth century, Maria, now in her late thirties, was drinking so heavily she was attracting the attention of the authorities. In July 1903, Maria was taken to Holloway Prison for three days on a charge of criminally neglecting her children. Though the charge was for a single incident on 17 July, it was noted that several similar instances had already occurred.

Being in sole charge of her four youngest children (William, the smallest was 7, and all were under the age of 16), Maria, it was found, 'did neglect them in a manner likely to cause them unnecessary suffering and injury to their health'. No more details of the case were given, save for a single explanatory sentence: 'Being a habitual drunkard.' Maria pleaded guilty to the charge.

There is no evidence that Maria was convicted as a drunkard prior to this event, but she was clearly known to the local courts. Individuals suffering with alcoholism were undoubtedly far more common than conviction rates show. Some families struggled for years with a relative who abused alcohol before the situation finally reached a crisis point and outside agencies became involved. For others, no one outside of the household might ever have known of a problem with alcoholism.

On 8 August that same year, Maria again came to the attention of the authorities, and this time her situation was felt serious enough to warrant her being sent to an inebriates home for three years – the longest sentence a magistrate could impose. Maria was released from the institution in 1906, and returned to North London and her family. Unfortunately, a relapse to drinking soon followed, and eighteen months later, in April 1908, Charles began proceedings to legally separate from Maria.

The formal separation of a married couple, although a decades-old practice, was still not a common occurrence. A separation required husband and wife to appear in front of a magistrate to state their case in a very public setting. The intimate problems of a marriage could become public knowledge, and at a time when a family's respectability was still jealously guarded, separation was not a step to take lightly. Charles was granted a separation from Maria on the grounds that she was a habitual drunkard, although Charles was still required to pay a weekly living allowance of 8s. to Maria.

Surprisingly, it was the loss of her husband, children and home that seems to have driven Maria to alter her behaviour, rather than the intervention of the courts or her three-year incarceration. In the two years that followed, Maria managed to reduce her drinking and to reconcile with Charles. By 1911, she was back living with him and their two youngest children. In the years that followed Maria did not appear in court again, or on a register as a habitual drunkard. She remained living with Charles until her death in 1920.

Chapter 32

MARY FITZPATRICK

(C. 1855 LEEDS) – CONVICT

Mary Corcoran was born in Leeds, Yorkshire, sometime between 1855 and 1858. Her parents were both migrants from famine-torn Ireland. Her father, Richard, worked as a greengrocer's labourer; her mother, Catherine, had no listed occupation, although she may have worked in one of the many casual occupations open to women at this time.

The Corcorans were a poor family struggling to make ends meet. This was a struggle that intensified as Mary's younger brother and sister were born, and the number of mouths to feed grew. From her early teens, Mary worked as a mill hand in a Leeds factory, which was a hard and dangerous job for a child. The Corcorans were devout Roman Catholics, and placed great emphasis on maintaining themselves as a religious family, and, despite their poverty, a respectable family too. There are no recorded offences for Mary, her parents or her siblings during their time living as a family unit.

At around the age of 18, Mary married Thomas Fitzpatrick, an Irish immigrant and labourer living in Leeds. The pair settled in the city and had two children. Yet within a few years, outside the supervision of her family, Mary began drinking, and her behaviour became increasingly difficult to manage. In March 1879, Mary was convicted at Leeds Police Court of being 'riotous' and sentenced to seven days in prison. Her conviction for riot would, in all likelihood, have led to Mary losing her job. Later that same year, Mary was reconvicted at York for stealing flannel and she was sentenced to four months' imprisonment. A few months later she was convicted of stealing handkerchiefs and given another two months' imprisonment.

Mary Fitzpatrick Courtesy of TNA, PCOM4; Piece: 65; Item: 18.

In June 1880, Mary spent another two months in prison for the theft of a hat and a scarf. Upon release, Mary narrowly avoided a conviction for burglary, despite being found hiding under a bed at the crime scene. With a string of convictions now behind her, Mary was under police supervision. She was known to local constables, who had the power to apprehend her if they suspected she was about to commit a crime or was not making an honest living. Mary was apprehended in this way in September of 1880, and spent seven days in prison simply for being a 'suspect person'.

With the police watching her closely, Mary's opportunity to offend was dramatically reduced. She managed to stay out of trouble for more than a year following her last period in prison. However, Mary's increasingly chaotic mode of living put considerable strain on her marriage and from 1881 Thomas and Mary were living apart.

In 1882, Mary's actions altered the course of both her and Thomas's lives forever. Mary, whom a judge later chastised for 'leading the life of a common person, and walking about the streets and drinking with men', was indicted in September 1882 with the wilful murder of James Richardson, a local glass blower. Richardson had met Mary after a day out drinking in numerous pubs in Leeds. Mary was the last person to be seen with Richardson alive, shortly before his body was found in a local mill dam. Mary was quickly linked to the case, having pawned a distinctive watch and chain Richardson had been seen with on the day of his death. Though Mary protested her innocence of the crime of murder, she evidently knew something of Richardson's demise. When apprehended by a constable, Mary was reported to have anxiously asked 'What am I going to be charged with?' Mary, in the month leading to her trial, continued to protest that Richardson had given her the watch as a gift. Thomas, unnerved by the thought that his wife (although estranged) was going to be tried for murder, quickly emigrated to America.

Ultimately, there was not enough evidence to convict on a murder charge, and Mary was found not guilty. She was then immediately tried on the lesser charge of robbery with violence, the prosecution alleging that Richardson died in a robbery gone wrong. In the end, the jury were only able to convict Mary for stealing from the person (still a serious crime, but unlikely to gain the same length of sentence as murder or violent robbery). Whilst they declared themselves satisfied that she had taken the goods, they felt there was simply not proof of how much violence, if any, had been used. The judge in passing sentence declared that Mary's history of convictions would stand against her, and that she could expect a more severe sentence than he would otherwise have given. Mary was sent to prison for six years' penal servitude. She left the dock still protesting her innocence, and calling out for her father.

In prison, Mary wrote fervently to her parents, and to anyone that would hear her protestations of innocence. In the third year of her sentence, shortly before she became eligible for release on licence, Mary asked to write to her husband in America, and the prison facilitated this contact.

Mary was released from convict prison to the East End Refuge in Fulham in 1886. Her parents had left Leeds whilst she had been in prison, and so she began making plans for a new beginning, rather than return home. With the help of one of many prisoners' aid charities, Mary journeyed to America to be reunited with her husband. At the age of 30, Mary had left Britain, and her former life, behind. With a clean slate and her life ahead of her, we can hope that she managed to leave offending behind too.

Chapter 33

ARABELLA MATILDA HOPTON

(B. 1862 GLOUCESTERSHIRE) – CONVICT

Arabella Huggins was born in 1862 in Barton St Mary in Gloucestershire. She was the eldest of the eight children of Edwin and Arabella. Her father worked as a plumber and glazier, a living generous enough to mean that she and her sisters, even in their late teens, were not required to undertake work.

In 1884, at the age of 23, she married local butcher Daniel Hopton, the son of a blacksmith. The first of their five children, a daughter Lilian, was born less than a year later. For almost two decades, the Hoptons lived an ordinary and respectable working-class existence. Daniel worked as both a butcher and a baker and presumably earnt enough to prevent Arabella taking on formal paid employment. Daniel died in 1900, leaving Arabella responsible for the financial care of their three remaining daughters (Arabella's two youngest children died in infancy). While 16-year-old Lilian and 14-year-old Violet took work as factory machinists, Arabella took work as a 'monthly nurse', allowing her still to care for 4-year-old Hilda.

'Monthly nurse' was the term used to describe the work of women who provided gynaecological care to others. This might mean helping during times of illness and menstruation, or assisting during pregnancy and childbirth. Women who worked in this capacity did not need any formal qualifications or experience. Most were older women, mothers themselves, and individuals that had spent years, if not decades, assisting friends and relatives in this manner. Arabella, a mother and eldest child, would likely have assisted others giving birth from an early age. She claimed to have been working (we must assume on an 'as and when' basis) as a midwife from at least 1893.

Certified midwives at the turn of the twentieth century.

Nursing was an obvious trade for women needing to earn a living in their forties, fifties and sixties but who had little or no experience of industrial work.

Arabella began officially practising midwifery in July 1902, when she became one of the first women to pass the Certified Midwives Board Examination. The Midwives Act of 1902 made provision for the professionalisation of midwifery in England and Wales. Amongst other things, the Act required all practising midwives to be officially certified, imposed penalties for those who were not and created a way of monitoring the profession. Arabella was enrolled on the list of certified midwives in 1904, where she remained for almost a decade. The formal roll was not only about recognising the professional capacity of women's work, but also, more importantly, about regulating it. For centuries women had been working informally as midwives, and this had allowed unsafe and unregulated practices to flourish. The roll not only provided details of trained midwives, it also kept records of malpractice by midwives.

153

The next decade was a time of relative stability for the Hopton family. Though her daughters married and moved on, Arabella remained living at the family home in Blenheim Road, Gloucester, and was even able to hire a domestic servant. Like many midwives who sympathised with the plight of the women they served, Arabella not only aided women in birth, she also offered to undertake abortion procedures for a fee. For performing these 'off record' operations, Arabella was struck off the Certified Midwives Roll in 1914, and she was no longer allowed to practise as a midwife. However, now well-known to women in the local community, she continued to offer her services and attend births. She did so in partnership with a registered nurse, Alice Sinclair. For a part of Arabella's fee, Sinclair would sign forms of birth and death for confinements that Arabella attended. The partnership came unstuck when the death of a baby in July 1915 revealed the fraudulent arrangements, and Arabella narrowly avoided prosecution. Despite this near-miss, Arabella riskily continued to provide illegal abortions.

The war years were an especially busy time for those practising abortions. Women who found themselves pregnant after adulterous relationships, or whose husbands had died on active service when they were pregnant, might seek out the services of a midwife or a nurse who offered this service when ordinarily they would never have thought of taking this course of action. There was also a standing pool of clients amongst young unmarried women, and those with large families who could not afford another mouth to feed. It was not until the 1920s that some limited forms of contraception were available, and even then they were limited to married women and difficult to obtain.

Arabella managed to be re-admitted to the midwives roll in 1920, but just months later, her illicit activities led to catastrophic events. Arabella had performed an abortion on Edith Barbara Watts, using a surgical instrument to procure a miscarriage. However, while the foetus had been damaged, a full miscarriage had not occurred. Watts soon developed septicaemia, and was admitted to a hospital where the dead foetus was removed. Unfortunately, the intervention was too late for Watts, who went into septic shock and died shortly afterwards. The cause of death was found to be a result of a dirty instrument used in the initial procedure carried out by Arabella. In this period abortions were primarily carried out at home with household items, often those who operated had no way of surgically sterilising their instruments and simply cleaned them with soap and water between patients.

Arabella was soon identified as the culprit and a case was built against her. Several other women came forward to testify to receiving similar procedures from her, despite her daughter and brother trying to put pressure on witnesses to withdraw testimony. It was noted that Arabella's procedures cost 5s. a time, and came with the strict condition that those who underwent them were not to reveal her identity or practice. The illegal trade in abortions involved considerable risk on both sides, one physical and one legal. Despite it being her first offence, Arabella was tried for the murder of Watts, and found guilty of a lesser charge of using an instrument to procure an abortion and sentenced to seven years' imprisonment. She served five years in a Liverpool prison before she was released in July 1925.

Where Arabella went after her discharge from prison is not entirely clear. It was not until almost four years later in 1929 that electoral rolls show her living with her family back in Gloucester. Now more than 60, and almost certainly disqualified from any further work as a midwife, Arabella would have had limited means for making her own living, and may well have been wary of continuing to practise the trade in illegal abortions, due to the heavy penalty she was likely to endure if another procedure went wrong.

As the Second World War broke out, Arabella was living with her daughter Hilda, and son-in-law William Hyett, next door to her elder daughter Violet. She earned her keep in this quiet suburb of Gloucester through unpaid domestic labour. Arabella continued to live with her family into her old age. Arabella was more than 90 when she died in early 1955, thirty years after her release from prison.

Chapter 34

SARAH DAVIES

(B. 1852 LLANELLI) – CONVICT

S arah Davies was born in Llanelli, Carmarthenshire, in 1852. Her father David ran the Collier's Arms public house in Llanelli, where he lived with the rest of the family. The family were respectable, with nothing known about them by the police save that Sarah's father had on one occasion been convicted for drunkenness. Sarah's pathway into offending is not particularly clear. Though she and her siblings grew up and established their own lives, the family seems to have stayed living in Carmarthenshire and they were in relatively close contact throughout their lives, with Sarah corresponding with her father, sister Rachel, aunt and cousin even during her imprisonment. What we do know is that, by the age of around 15, Sarah was already frequenting the streets and working as a prostitute. However, her first conviction was not for prostitution or disorderly behaviour, but for theft. She was prosecuted for stealing a gown and sentenced to six weeks in Swansea Prison with hard labour. In fact, Sarah was never convicted for prostitution-related offences, or for drunkenness or disorderly and violent behaviour like so many other young women in her position.

In 1867 she was in court again, this time for the theft of a duck. Sarah maintained her innocence and the case was eventually dismissed. The woman who alleged the theft was a brothel-keeper. Although the truth of the incident is lost to time, it was not unknown for brothel-keepers to bring prosecutions for theft against the girls that lived and worked for them as a form of discipline. A month later, Sarah was back in court, this time at the Swansea Sessions, and she was given six months in prison with hard labour for the theft of a petticoat.

Matilda Bramble (alias Sarah Davies). Courtesy of TNA, PCOM4; Piece: 65; Item: 3.

Theft was not Sarah's primary occupation. Many months and even years lapsed between her convictions, during which time Sarah made her living as a prostitute, though lack of convictions would suggest that this was neither a daily trade, nor one carried out on the street. Sarah also worked at one time as a factory hand, though this employment was short lived. In March 1871 Sarah was back to prison for two months' hard labour for the theft of a shawl: she was captured on the census in a small local prison holding her and just forty-two other women. Two years later in October 1873 she was again convicted of stealing, this time dress-maker's material, and given eighteen months' hard labour.

Over the course of two decades, Sarah used a range of different names to identify herself. The name of Sarah Davies was a common one in Llanelli, the county of Carmarthen, and south Wales. If her primary aim was evading detection, keeping her own name may have been a better way than the range of flamboyant aliases she used. The two most frequently used were Matilda Bramble and Letitia Power – much easier names for the police to remember and trace. We can perhaps infer that the aliases she adopted were not (or at the very least not solely) about trying to evade capture, but about creating an identity that she felt more suited her sense of self.

With four previous offences behind her, Sarah's criminal record was beginning to become a problematic factor for her in trials. Her 1873 sentence was a full year longer than any previous sentence, and illustrated that judges were beginning to identify her as a serious offender. Not long after her release from prison in 1875, Sarah was again put on trial, this time at the Cardiff Sessions for the theft of a jacket, and this time, her luck ran out. She was sentenced to seven years of penal servitude and transported to a convict prison in London.

Apart from occasional minor disobedience – singing in her cell, illicitly communicating with other prisoners, verbally abusing the staff and refusing to obey orders – Sarah passed her time in convict prison quietly. She was released to the Russell House Refuge in July 1879, around halfway through her sentence. She had kept in touch with her friends and family in Wales, and returned there as soon as her time in the refuge was up. Unfortunately for Sarah, on licence and under police supervision, when she stole a coat not long after returning, she was swiftly apprehended and put on trial at the Swansea Sessions the next day. She returned to convict prison for another seven years. Not only would she be required to serve her new sentence, she also had more than a year of her old sentence from which she had been licensed left to serve as well.

Sarah's prison record indicates a desperation to get out of prison almost as soon as she returned. Not only was her behaviour much improved, with only one incident of damage to prison property and one incident of receiving food from another prisoner, but she began petitioning for release as soon as she was able. In 1884, aware that she would soon be eligible for early release, Sarah began making enquiries with the prison authorities about emigration schemes for released convicts. She wrote she was 'anxious to emigrate to avoid bad associates'. Emigration of ex-offenders was looked on favourably by the prison service, and the wheels for her release began turning

Upon her release from prison the following year, having served almost a decade in prison with only a small glimpse of freedom in the middle, Sarah decided to cut her losses. Life back in Carmarthenshire was not working well for her. Her last experience of release from convict prison, burdened by police supervision, had taught her that it was only too easy to slip straight back into old habits. On the day of her discharge, Sarah went straight to the Discharged Prisoners' Aid Society at Charing Cross, where arrangements were made for her imminent travel to America.

There are no records for Sarah in America, but of course, on arrival, she may have changed names again, and taken on a brand-new identity she felt more fitting for her brand-new life.

Chapter 35

JANE FOSTER

(C.1822 SOMERBY, LINCS) – LOCAL PRISONER

Those who led the most precarious economic lives were those most vulnerable to arrest. They were, however, also those least likely to consistently appear in the official record. Without well-ingrained support networks and stable residential arrangements, those working in informal, temporary or insecure employments could all too easily find themselves at the mercy of the streets. There they slipped from the grasp of many social records. Accounts of the crimes and trials of such individuals are sometimes the only insight we get into their largely undocumented lives.

Jane was born in Somersby, Lincolnshire, between 1818 and 1825. More than a decade before mandatory national registrations, we cannot be precisely sure of the date, and it appears, neither was Jane, who variously reported her age to suggest that her date of birth was 1820, 1818, 1823, 1824 and 1826. Jane was born in South Lincolnshire, but moved further north to Sleaford searching for work. She was already married and 30 years old when our period begun, having married James Foster in 1843.

James, like Jane, had few marketable skills, and struggled to find secure well-paying employment. The pair began working as hawkers. James was licensed to do so, Jane was not. The living afforded them was enough to survive, but not to find anywhere permanent to live, or to establish a stable life. The pair began living increasingly precariously, sometimes lodging, but often sleeping rough as they moved from place to place around Lincoln and the surrounding towns.Despite their irregular mode of life, Jane seems to have avoided being convicted for any offences for more than a decade.

Victorian street-sellers in Covent Garden.

However, by the time she did appear in court in 1860, charged with being drunk and incapable, she was obviously already known to the police, and it was noted at her trial that she 'was said to be connected to a gang of thieves'. Street-sellers, like beggars and prostitutes, spent long hours waiting in public spaces with little to do. On days of slow trade, and in cold inclement weather, alcohol provided a cheap and easy source of entertainment. Unfortunately, the public nature of their lives meant that even relatively harmless acts of drunkenness or rowdy socialising (the likes of which occurred in pubs throughout Britain) could quickly be classified as a breach of public order.

Things worsened for Jane and James after the birth of their son, John, in 1868. Their financial strain was only intensified by the needs of a child. While they did not relinquish custody of John, they did sporadically place him in the workhouse when Jane was in prison, or safe accommodation was lacking. It is not clear whether during these times Jane and James always stayed together, or went to different parts of the country to try and raise funds. Jane was certainly known locally as a vagrant, and although she always gave her marital status as married, she always appeared alone in court, and used the aliases of Robinson and Kendal. By 1881 Jane, James and John were living together again in a cramped court dwelling along with twenty-seven other people.

Not all of Jane's apprehensions led to convictions. As a vagrant or 'tramp' when she was picked up by the police for drunkenness, Jane might only be confined in the police station or local lock-up for a night, giving her a chance to sober up before she was released and encouraged to move on. Often it was more useful for local police to move a vagrant on than it was to prosecute them and begin a cycle of reconviction which kept troubled individuals in the local area. Jane's custodial sentences were primarily a result of her petty thefts. In the 1880s, as Jane entered her sixties, the thefts she may already have been carrying out for the majority of her life became clumsier and easier to detect.

Between 1880 and 1890 Jane had more than thirteen convictions for theft, earning her between one week and three months' hard labour. Jane started out by stealing large items of clothing like coats and gowns, but changed tactics to steal items that could less conspicuously be sold on the street – items such as hairbrushes, cigarette cases, spectacles and books. She also stole consumable items like food which once sold and eaten left no trace of a crime.

At the end of April 1891 Jane was arrested for taking a basket belonging to a neighbour, Mrs Jones. The basket had been lent to Jane several times before by Jones for work, and always returned. However, on this occasion Jane had taken the basket without asking.

Whether she genuinely intended to steal the basket or not was uncertain, though her record of previous convictions spoke against her. Jane had been in prison on remand for ten weeks awaiting the trial, and was sentenced to a further two months of imprisonment. Life was becoming harder, and selling anything on the street without attracting police attention more impossible.

In June 1894 Jane was sentenced to six months' imprisonment for theft, with a term of two years' police supervision attached. She was released in December that year, and managed to avoid reconviction for almost a year, until September 1895, when she received another month. As she was under police supervision, it is likely that Jane refrained from offending in the first three-quarters of 1895. However, with stealing constituting a vital part of her income, Jane was plunged into considerable poverty by attempting to stay on the right side of the law. On discharge at the end of 1894, having spent six months on the Wakefield Prison diet, Jane's build was described as 'proportional' and her face 'round', By September 1895, having struggled to subsist, her build had altered to 'slender', her face drawn and 'long'.

In 1897, when she was sentenced to seven days of hard labour for being drunk and disorderly, the *Lincolnshire Free Press* reported that 'she has already spent twenty years of her life in prison, seven days hard labour is but a modest addition to such a record'. Jane had never been given a sentence longer than a few months of imprisonment, most of her sentences were just a few days in length. To have accumulated twenty years in custody illustrates just how frequently Jane found herself picked up from streets and prosecuted.

Given the hardships of Jane's life, her frequent homelessness, more than twenty years spent undertaking the harsh regime of local prisons and the scarce availability of food and medical care, it is quite remarkable that, after her last release from prison, Jane survived another ten years, and died at the age of nearly 90 in 1907.

Part 3

HOW TO RESEARCH

Chapter 36

WOMEN'S CRIMES

From murder to picking pockets, from street robbery to prostitution, the crimes that a woman committed are often one of the most intriguing parts of her story. The courtroom was the place in which details of a woman's offences, and the circumstances from which they arose, were explored. Although they were diffuse and sporadic, records of trials and the remarkable testimony given by police officers, witnesses and even offenders themselves, can be found in numerous places.

Interest in the dark underbelly of British society peaked in our period. Alongside official records of crime, a number of intrepid 'social investigators' made successful careers from writing down all they discovered about crime and criminals from interviews, observations and from ethnographic research (living amongst the poor and working classes). A few remarkable offenders themselves even wrote autobiographies or memoirs about their criminal careers and time in prison. This chapter looks through a few of the key sources that can tell us not just the 'what' and 'when' of crime but also, wherever possible, the 'how', 'where' and 'why' of women's offending too.

KEY DOCUMENTS

Police Courts and Assize Court Registers made a record of every trial that took place in England and Wales during our period. For higher courts, comprehensive records exist and they note the date and place of trial, the name of a defendant, category of crime (though not details), verdict and sentence. The Criminal Registers of England and Wales are most accessible for the period 1792 to 1892. Police court records performed a similar function. However petty sessions registers usually contained a little more information. Along with the above data, they also often recorded the age of a defendant, the name of the victim or complainant on whose behalf they were being prosecuted, the number of previous court appearances and even the address of the defendant. Unfortunately, most petty sessions registers, thought to be of little interest and a burden to store, were often destroyed a few decades after their creation. Some do survive, but the locations and years which they cover are sporadic at best.

British newspapers offer us so much more than court records when it comes to the detail of a crime. The report of a woman's appearance in court will often not only come with the name of a defendant, the date of the offence, but also multiple details of the nature of the offence and the sentence. Reports often give us a ready-formed narrative of the context of the crime. Instead of simply telling us a woman was convicted of simple larceny, a report will usually specify that it was child-stripping (taking clothes from children), shoplifting or theft from the local market. The report might say what goods were taken, who the victim was, where and when the crime was carried out. In cases of particular interest, reports can also come with a potted life or criminal history for the individual on trial, or snippets of information about their personal life (children, illegitimacy, bereavements, personal relationships) which are of great value in identify and tracing offenders in subsequent records.

However, although the newspapers have the potential to tell us so much about individuals and their crimes in rich detail, they do not provide comprehensive coverage of the daily police courts. The papers would only report a proportion of the cases that were heard in each session. Court reporters would usually select only those that were most newsworthy. This might mean cases that had garnered local or national attention or spoke to current social attitudes, or concerns, or which were thought to be good entertainment for readers – crimes involving colourful characters, or with outbursts in court, or perhaps a crime with an interesting angle. While lots of offenders were recorded somehow in the newspapers, press coverage became a self-fulfilling cycle which overrepresented certain types of offenders. The more an offender became 'known', the more likely a report on their case would appear in the paper; the more press coverage they received, the more newsworthy they became. Those criminal women with just one or two convictions for petty larceny were far less likely to have their cases reported than the habitual drunkard with eighty-odd offences. Researchers should take note that, just because a woman cannot be found in the newspaper court reports, it does not mean a trial did not take place. This is why it is essential to use newspapers in conjunction with other sources when we are trying to uncover narratives of women's lives.

Assize transcripts allow an unparalleled glimpse into the higher level courtroom, and surviving Ordinary's accounts can even take us all the way to the gallows (the Ordinary of Newgate was the clergyman at Newgate Prison who wrote down some offenders' life-stories). Records of major courts and circuits like the Old Bailey in London and the Northern and North Eastern Assize in Yorkshire provide the opportunity to learn about the crime and punishment taking place in some of England's higher courts. Transcriptions of cases, created as they were heard, give us an almost complete record of the evidence presented to the judge and jury. Transcripts are by far the most comprehensive records of any court case and show us the circumstances and context of crime in fine detail (although they are rarely a complete record of everything said in court). They also offer the chance to get a feel for court life and for how offenders, prosecutors and witnesses told the story of offending in their own words.

Contemporary accounts and prisoner autobiographies are a great place to start for those wishing to know more about life for poor and working women and the landscape of crime in this era. Whether looking for information which will provide a context to the life of a specific individuals, or seeking to get a feel for a period, place or experience before archival research begins, writings from contemporaries are a fantastic resource. The writings of so-called 'social investigators' like Henry Mayhew and Beatrice and Sidney Webb sought to reveal the largely hidden lives of the impoverished, destitute and marginal in nineteenth- and early twentieth-century Britain. Mayhew is credited with interviewing hundreds of beggars, vagrants, drunks, prostitutes and petty criminals in his career as a journalist and investigator. These works remain some of the only first-person accounts of crime in our period. Likewise, the Victorian fascination with crime and the underworld meant that prison biographies, written by offenders and former prison inmates, became popular reading. Autobiographies, although rare, do exist, and are one of the few sources we have in which criminal women tell their own stories at length.

ACCESSING RECORDS

All of the materials that we have discussed in the sections above are available to access in either hard copy or digitally, and most have both access options. While subscription sites can offer the most convenient way for researchers to access material, all the records are available for free in some format.

The British Library has the UK's largest collection of historic newspapers, with more than 34,000 different titles from around the globe, and more than 60,000,000 individual issues. The collections range from the seventeenth century up until publications for the present day. The collection includes thousands of newspapers printed during the period 1850 to 1925 from national and local papers printed throughout the British Isles. Newspapers can be accessed from the British Library Reading Room in St Pancras, and in Boston Spa,

Illustrated London News.

West Yorkshire. Newspapers are available (depending on condition of original material) to view in hard copy and on microfilm, if the title and issue of the paper is known. Of course it is not possible to keyword search original material, and so readers looking to carry out a search for a named individual, or reports of a particular crime may be better off using the British Newspaper Archive, the online service currently holding more than 600 British titles, and 14,000,000 individual pages of news. The digital service is free to use on site at the British Library, and in many other large libraries.

Newspapers can be searched for keywords, and phrases such as 'She was a returned convict', 'Factory worker' or 'Irish girl', and be combined with article titles to help reduce potential results. Reports of the police court were almost always printed under one of a handful of subtitles, like 'Police Intelligences', 'Police Court' or 'Police News'. In locations such as London with more than one magistrates' court sitting every day, the name of the court itself might need to be used (if the area is known). For example, those wishing to search for crime by Irish women in Westminster might search 'Irish woman' AND 'Police Intelligence' AND 'Westminster' to return the relevant pages. It is the same when researching Australian courts: Sydney had two police courts from quite early in its settlement for example.

The Newspaper Archive (www.britishnewspaperarchives.co.uk) is available for those researching remotely to access for a fee. Digitised newspapers are an invaluable resource for those seeking to trace offenders as we have done here. The coverage of digitised newspapers across the UK is fairly good, with several titles for each county. However, researchers conducting studies of women in a particular area may prefer to consult the full archive at the British Library, or in their local library/local studies centre, which will probably have multiple titles for each locality.

For those researching transported women, the Trove database (www.trove.nla.gov.au) of Australian newspapers contains more than two hundred years of newspaper coverage from the colony of Tasmania alone, and is completely free to access.

Archive.org is a free internet archive where millions of historic books and publications (alongside audio and visual recordings, software and websites) are available to download, in a variety of formats, free of charge. Searches can be made by keyword, title and author of the work, and can be restricted by a number of other criteria. Works by Henry Mayhew, Jack London, Florence Maybrick and William Booth are all available to download. We make further reading suggestions for prisoners' autobiographies and memoirs, and social investigators' works at the back of this book. The archive also contains hundreds of copies of periodicals and monthly publications useful for the study of crime, for example, the *Illustrated London News*. However, the texts themselves cannot be keyword searched, and so researchers should approach the collections ready to browse.

Old Bailey Online

Copies of the original printed transcriptions of the Old Bailey Proceedings can be found at the British Library, the Guildhall Library in London, and Harvard University Library, though the full collection of this material is available at www.oldbaileyonline.org.

For more than a decade the Proceedings of the Old Bailey have been available to access free of charge online. The text of each proceeding has been digitised and tagged by creators in order to produce a fully searchable database. The website provides a sophisticated search facility allowing not only keyword searching, but also name searching, the option to select particular dates, offences, or punishments. Users can also specify whether they are looking for defendants, victims, or witnesses to a particular offence. When researching individual criminal women, name searches are the most useful, but those who want to conduct broader research into female offending or particular crimes carried out by women might find the keyword search particularly useful. Keyword searches in conjunction with other fields like date and offence can produce fascinating results about the nature and context of women's offences. For example, the use of place and street names, contextual items such as gin or beer, knives or fire pokers, and even colloquial terms for offences like prostitution, can reveal a rich world of female offending often obscured from formal reporting.

Local Archives

Local archives for the county in which women lived can contain many surviving petty sessions records, though researchers will be disappointed to find that these can be few and far between. The London Metropolitan Archives has particularly good police court holdings for certain London courts. Local archives will usually also have microfilmed newspapers published specifically for the area in which they circulated, many of which have not been digitised by the British Library, and can contain much more thorough reporting of crime and disorder in a particular parish or town.

STRENGTHS AND LIMITATIONS

Newspapers, social investigation and trial reports reveal some of the most important details it takes to turn a list of offences into a life-story. One of the greatest strengths of newspaper reports about crime are that, unlike other sources, they were often actively seeking to record the voices of criminal women, voices that society, and history, have long kept quiet.

Any printed source telling us about crime is subject to three factors which mean information is misreported, missing or incorrectly filed, all of which can cause problems for researchers. The first and most recent limitation of these sources, particularly in the case of digitised records, is that the very process of curating them changes or misrepresents the content. While the Optical Character Recognition software used to digitise masses of print newspapers is usually of a high quality, the poor quality of some original documents can lead to misreading. Letters become jumbled or replaced by incorrect characters, and certain results become unsearchable. Thus some names will return no search results despite relevant newspaper results existing.

The other limitation with the sources is in the content of the text itself. Records like the Old Bailey provide the most accurate reporting of what happened in a court room, but even they contain omissions. Testimony in court was often obtained then, as now, through a series of questions and answers. However, while the Old Bailey shows us the response of victims, witnesses, and defendants, the text did not record the question asked, making it in many cases hard to understand the information we are being given. Newspapers similarly contain a selection bias of the information editors chose to report from trials (though it must be said that newspapers contain a far greater bias than records like the Old Bailey Proceedings). Editors regularly chose to highlight certain factors or testimony in a case that fit a narrative they were trying to tell, be in comedic, tragic or moral. While the information contained in court reports is no less fascinating or valid on account of editorial bias, they should, nonetheless, be interpreted as a representation of events, rather than an objective account. The same stands true for the writings of social investigators who, despite many good intentions, were trying to tell a good story.

The final (and first) stage at which mistruths and inaccuracies creep into accounts of crime is in the testimony of offenders themselves. Women on trial had many motives for telling the stories they did. Some were no doubt truthful in their recounting of the circumstances of their lives and the events that led them to the dock. Others will have been attempting, like the newspapers that wrote about them, to tell a particular kind of story about their lives, perhaps trying to elicit sympathy from those that listened, or settle ongoing scores with friends and neighbours. There were also those who would tell any number of mistruths to cover up personal details they did not want publicly known, or simply to escape prosecution. The testimony of criminal women themselves is some of the best evidence we can hope to find, but we should always remember that those on trial might not tell 'the truth, the whole truth, and nothing but the truth'.

We can find a great deal of information about the specific activities that saw women put on trial by looking both inside and outside the courtroom. Registers help us to get a sense of the frequency and nature of the crimes women committed, although there are less surviving records for lower courts, at which women were most commonly convicted, than we might like. However, it is the reports of trials, rather than the formal log of them that give us our greatest insight into women's lives and how they broke the law. In court transcripts and newspaper reports we are given the opportunity to learn the details of crime – the weapons used, the items stolen, the disturbance caused and the names and details of the victims and co-offenders. It is often in these reports that we might learn for the first time of the circumstances of a woman's life that saw her resort to crime, from illegitimate children and battles with alcohol, to marital disputes and work in the sex-trade. The work of social investigators too can be invaluable for learning more about the hidden world in which the individuals we seek lived. Despite the issues of bias in reporting and the reliability of testimony, both in hard copy and print, sources reporting the details of women's offences and trials are some of the most important documents available when it comes to narrating the lives of criminal women.

Chapter 37

HOW TO RESEARCH: WOMEN AND THE 'EXPERIENCE' OF IMPRISONMENT

At the start of the twenty-first century a large number of prisons were decommissioned, and 're-purposed'. Reading Prison, for example, which opened in 1844, closed in 2013. Designed by George Gilbert Scott and based on the New Model Prison at Pentonville, it has now been converted into a theatre and community arts centre (complete with exhibition about its former role, and celebrity inmates such as Oscar Wilde). Northallerton's conversion is part of a new civic centre. It incorporates the prison's five listed buildings which includes two female wings built in the 1800s and the governor's block. HMPs Dorchester, Gloucester, Kingston, Portsmouth, and Shepton Mallet have all been sold to a development company. Shrewsbury Prison hosts funded 'escape' role-play sessions, but in the long term will be redeveloped for housing. Oxford Castle is now a high-class hotel. HMP Canterbury has recently been sold to Christchurch University and there are plans to turn the Georgian and Victorian parts of the estate into student accommodation, potentially with a heritage centre attached. Many other decommissioned prisons, however, have been turned into museums of punishment. This chapter takes four former sites of incarceration and trial in Ireland, Wales, England and Australia, to see how the convict past is marketed, and asks what we as researchers can gain as a result of visiting gaol museums? Through visiting these museums, is it possible to experience what life was like for female prisoners?

175

The bureaucratic record.

KEY SOURCES

Kilmainham Prison, Dublin, was originally built in 1796, but was remodelled on many occasions. In the early nineteenth century, there was no segregation of prisoners, with men, women and children all held together in poorly lit, unheated cells. Conditions for women prisoners were persistently worse than for men, and eventually prompted some redevelopment. That did not substantially alter conditions for female prisoners however, and they remained in cramped overcrowded accommodation in the 1840s. It got worse when the Irish Famine brought in a great influx of prisoners. In the twentieth century, many women who took part in the 1916 rising were imprisoned in Kilmainham and more than three hundred were imprisoned there during the Irish Civil War. The prison was then decommissioned in the 1920s. In the 1950s a preservation society, the Kilmainham Gaol Restoration Society, was formed. The prison reopened as a museum in the late 1960s and the final restoration of the site was completed in 1971. The museum regularly hosts exhibitions about the history of Irish nationalism, and provides guided prison tours. In 2013, there was an exhibition of bonnets, representing many of the convict women transported to Australia. Between 2012 and 2014 the prison hosted a project which identified, photographed and analyszed the surviving graffiti in the West Wing of the prison. The exhibition was designed to aid public understandings of female experiences of imprisonment. Because there are no surviving prison records for the women in the prison, the Kilmainham Gaol Graffiti project created alphabetised lists – one in English and one in Irish – of the women who put their names to autograph books and on the walls (whilst imprisoned and on return visits in the years after the prison had been decommissioned). The women's names, home addresses and prison addresses can be found on the project website (https://kilmainhamgaolgraffiti.com). In this way, following a visit, and the experience of 'being inside', visitors can follow up the names and lives of the women in documents held in local archives. That way we experience the lives of female prisoners from an informed as well as an emotional perspective.

Similar attempts to help visitors experience 'incarceration' have also been made in Wales. Like many other prisons, Ruthin Gaol was decommissioned in the 1920s. The prison, which was designed on the Pentonville model, was reopened as a heritage attraction. Visitors can explore the cells, including the solitary confinement cell, and the place where condemned prisoners were held before execution. There are also opportunities to dress up in convict maid 'costume'. The gaol museum is popular, and is now an integral part of the heritage appeal of Denbighshire.

The Cascades Female Factory (http://femalefactory.org.au) is Australia's most significant historic site associated with female convicts. The 'factory' was intended to reform female convicts through work and discipline. Thousands of women and children were imprisoned here, and as the website reminds us, many died there due to high rates of illness and infant mortality. There are guided tours of the remains of the institution. Today the site consists of three of the original five yards. Most of the original buildings have been demolished or have fallen down, but the original footprint of the factory is still there. There is also a theatre show where actors portray life in the factory in 1833, in an attempt to convey the harshness of convict women's lives.

St George's Hall is the site of Liverpool's former Assize Court which was closed in 1956. Cases heard at the Assizes included serious offences which could result in a death sentence or transportation to Australia. Liverpool Assizes have witnessed some of the most famous trials in British history, including Florence Maybrick's trial in 1889. She was accused of poisoning her husband with arsenic, and, following conviction, was sentenced to death. Despite the huge interest in the case at the time, and long-lived historical interest, there is little mention of the Maybrick case in St George's Hall. The cells below court have been turned into a small exhibition, with some interpretation boards about the lives of women who passed through the court; but the Victorian Assize Court, which is magnificent, is allowed to speak for itself, with little interpretation being applied.

These are just four examples of the many gaol, police and court museums which have grown up around the world. Different approaches have been taken to preserve both the physical fabric, and the 'sense' of the institution. In some cases the buildings have been left relatively untouched – such as St George's Hall – in others, the buildings have been turned into a museum with exhibitions, reconstructions, dramatic renditions and so on. They are all designed to convey something of the atmosphere of the building, and, in the case of gaol museums, inform the public of the conditions endured by the women who were incarcerated within their walls.

ACCESSING RECORDS

If we want to find out more about the prisoners whose experiences the museums try to capture and re-present, records can be found in archives near the gaol museums. In the case of Ruthin Gaol, extremely near. Denbighshire Archive is part of the same redeveloped gaol complex as the museum (http://archives.denbighshire.gov.uk/about-us/), however, unfortunately, it does not hold many records relating to the prison. Most of what has survived about Ruthin is held at The National Archives (TNA). There are fifty-two records for 1800–1900 period, which include lists of prisoners, correspondence, and some administrative details. Women who were confined or convicted in Ruthin and were then released on licence can be found in the TNA, and in online collections. These include Margaret Davies, aged 52, who lived in Clwyd Street, Ruthin, and was convicted of receiving stolen goods (straw hats and dresses) on 4 July 1861; she was sentenced to four years's penal servitude, and was released on licence in 1864. Her full story can be found in the PCOM4 licences. Elizabeth Williams's story, on the other hand, can be found in HO 17/33/154. She worked as a dairy maid at Broughton Hall, near Hawarden, Wrexham, and was convicted on 17 May 1838 of the murder of her illegitimate infant son by drowning him in a fish pond. She was sentenced to death, but because of her good character and the sympathy of the jury she was recommended to mercy. Sixteen residents of Ruthin petitioned for her, and the files contain a petition from Samuel Sandbach, High Sheriff of Denbighshire, as well as a report of case with notes by Mr Justice Vaughan. She had her sentence commuted to five years' imprisonment and transportation for life.

Elizabeth was, of course, not the only woman sentenced to transportation. Some of the women who were imprisoned in the Cascades Female Factory when they arrived in Van Diemen's Land can be found in the Tasmanian Archives and Heritage Office (http://search.archives.tas.gov.au/Default.aspx). Within a well-established and very substantial collection on convicts, there are nearly a hundred documents about the Cascades, ranging from books, photographs, newspaper articles, biographies and modern published histories of the Factory.

As well as the cases being very well-reported in contemporary newspapers, the case files of women who were tried at Liverpool Assizes can be found in Liverpool Records Office located in the recently renovated City Library. The fifteen kilometres of archive holdings kept there preserve and provide access to a large and diverse collection of records. Many collections relate to women's history in Liverpool, which help to contextualise the lives of women in this period. For example, some of the women who appeared at the Assizes will have benefited from the Liverpool Rescue Society and House of Help (whose records are kept under the reference 362 HOU). The Society opened in 1890 to provide shelter for women and girls who had 'fallen into sin and to those hovering on the brink of ruin'. There was also the Liverpool branch of the Vigilance Association (reference M326 VIG) which was originally set up in 1908 to meet and help women and girls travelling through Liverpool who were vulnerable to exploitation (https://liverpool.gov.uk/libraries/archives-family-history/). Records like these are a timely reminder that much of the information we want to find on female prisoners actually resides in non-criminal record sources.

STRENGTHS AND LIMITATIONS

The advertising on the Cascades website suggests that 'Visiting the site today can be both emotional and rewarding, creating a connection with the stories of female convicts in Australia and their children – stories that are often tragic, but than also inspire hope and resilience'. Clearly the experience of visiting the Cascades is meant to transform opinion, and do more than educate visitors about the punishment of women two hundred years ago; it is designed to inspire, and relate to modern social issues. At Kilmainham too, there are wider socio-political themes being worked. Visiting physical sites of incarceration, punishment and trial can not only help bring the narratives of criminal women to life and, it can also help us explore the relevance of those stories to modern life and society, but can this really help us to 'experience' what women imprisoned there 'felt'?

The main emotions the imprisoned women felt were separation (from family, friends, society), loss of autonomy and loss of control over one's life, fear (from other prisoners or warders), weariness and hunger. Visitors today, according to comments on Trip Advisor, feel something different: 'went with the family, was very interesting, children got a Quiz sheet and could dress up and have a photo taken dressed as a criminal which was only £1 would recommend good place to visit' ... 'It is very cool in the cells so a pleasant place to visit if you want a break from the sun for a while'... 'We went here with family, my niece who was 8 loved it there was plenty of outfits for her to wear, we found it a little expensive for visit that didn't take very long'. The last comment is most telling. If we really want to experience what imprisonment was like, we would need to visit a gaol museum, find a cell and lock ourselves in there for ten years. We can only get a taste of what life was like for female convicts. While it may not be enough, it is the best we have. The alternative would be never to see inside these secret penal places, and not begin to understand the conditions and environments that female convicts endured.

The strengths of the gaol museums are that they play a vital part in helping us to confront things we would rather forget, and the emotional and physical journeys that the criminal women we research underwent. They remind us that prisoners were kept in awful conditions; secondly (and this is a feature of many gaol museums) they remind users that prisons today still separate people from their families, and are not 'holiday camps'. They are limited by the fact that they have to entertain as well as educate in order to attract visitors, and therefore they can tend to sensationalise particular aspects of imprisonment; we always have to remember, as well, that visiting prison museums can never completely recreate prison experiences, because we are free to leave at any time.

At their best, gaol and court museums shape opinion and challenge our understanding of prisoners' experiences. They can use the physical environment to reveal the experience of imprisonment which otherwise would remain hidden, or, if not hidden, not 'felt' as keenly. For example, it is easy to read about cramped, dark cells, but much easier to empathise with how imprisoned women felt when one is standing inside a small bleak whitewashed cell in Ruthin or Kilmainham; or standing in the windswept yard at Cascades. Visiting a gaol museum does help forge an emotional connection to the history of offenders which does not happen so often when reading archival documents.

The best approach to recapturing the 'experience' of a criminal woman is a mixed one. We can use the document created by the authorities to understand much of what women experienced inside prisons, or in inebriates homes and other carceral institutions, but it may not be until we step inside the former prisons themselves that we can begin to understand something about how they felt. The stench of prison-cooked cabbage and potatoes, other prisoners' sweaty bodies and the sounds of cell doors closing may be absent, but a visit to a gaol museum does help us to 'feel' the sense of containment and confinement that thousands of women suffered in the nineteenth century.

Chapter 38

HOW TO RESEARCH: WOMEN CONVICTS AND POST-SENTENCE SUPERVISION

When women walked out of the prison gates, what bureaucratic record did they leave behind, and what records would be kept on them in their first few days, months, and years of freedom? This chapter explores the convict caption documents (which are commonly known as prison licences, although they are only one part of sometimes voluminous sets of records), registers created by the habitual offender legislation enacted in 1869 and 1871, and some of the records of Discharged Prisoners' Societies, looking at Northumberland and South Staffordshire in particular. Together these documents contain a huge wealth of information about convict women, and this chapter unlocks their potential for readers to take advantage of in the future.

KEY SOURCES

Found in The National Archives (TNA) and online subscription sites PCOM 4 (Home Office and Prison Commission: Female Licences, 1853–1887) are the prison caption documents for female convicts. They were created when a convict entered their first institution, and continued to follow them around the various prisons in which they served their sentence. They were then held by the authorities until the convict was either released, or licensed. If the licence was revoked because the ex-convict had broken any of the conditions, or had been reconvicted, or if the ex-convict was subsequently sentenced to another period of penal servitude sometime later in their lives, more pages were added to the existing caption document. Eventually all the surviving documents were deposited in The National Archives. The surviving available caption documents for women run from 1853 to 1871 and 1882 to 1887. Many captions collected between 1870 and 1880, and the period after 1887, have been lost or destroyed.

The captions are made up of several parts. The *front-page* records: the name, age, religion, occupation, place of birth and last place of residence of the prisoner; name and address of next of kin; offence, place of conviction, sentence; and previous convictions. It also includes biometric data such as hair and eye colour, shape of face and body, and any marks, scars, tattoos or disfigurements. These details can be particularly useful to us when trying to identify a convict with a common name or many aliases in subsequent records, as in the case of Mary Gannon. Front sheets also contain details of the prisoner's height and weight every time they moved prisons in their sentence. As might be expected, height varies little (again very useful for identification), but weight does vary quite considerably, and can give us a window into how women fared under a prison diet. A woman gaining weight on the prison diet tells us a certain amount about her deprivation in outside life, as does weight loss in prison, which might indicate a reduced diet or illness.

Front matter is followed by the *medical sheet* which noted whether the convict had ever had syphilis, smallpox, scrofula or ulcers, whether she had been vaccinated against disease; and the general health of her main organs (lungs, heart and her mind). Then, every time someone was ill, spent time in the prison infirmary or was treated for disease, their complaint, weight and response to treatment were noted on the record. This is some of the only information researchers will ever have on the health of working women in the nineteenth century.

A mark sheet usually follows, showing a convict's progress in number of marks earned every week, this is accompanied by a record of each *prison offence* the convict committed, some of the details of the offence, and the punishment. For example, it might say that Julia Hyland was found guilty of speaking obscenely to a prison officer, threatening the Matron, breaking a window in her cell and singing during prayers (all very common 'infractions' of the regulations) for which she was punished with loss of marks that she had earned through her prison labour, a reduced diet and maybe some time in solitary confinement. A number of the women we have featured in this book suffered these punishments. Very few prisoners committed no 'offences' whilst in prison.

There is a record of accidents and injuries; petitions made for early release and so on; and a list of letters that the convict received, and letters that she sent out. These contain invaluable information about the names and addresses of friends and family, and can be of great use in identifying convicts in civil documents and future offences. Whenever a letter was sent out, the local police were charged with establishing if the recipient was making an honest living. Sometimes their assessment of whether the recipient (usually a friend or family member) was 'respectable', 'consorted with thieves' or 'a drunk' also lie in the folder, throwing an interesting light on the home environment and social networks, as least as perceived by the local constabulary. Quite often it is possible to determine whether the convict has been imprisoned in her own name or under an alias – quite a few letters start with 'in here, they know me as …'.

Lastly, the caption documents contain the *licence document*, signed by the Home Secretary (who must have worn out his quill given the number of women who were released early each year). From 1871 each licence has a photo 'mugshot' attached, the conditions that had to be adhered to, and the period of time that would have to be served if the licence was breached. Valuable research has been completed, using these records, to assess whether early release schemes were effective in this period (not least because the success or failure of the current system of early release is still hotly debated).

Most of these documents have been digitised and made available online for a fee, or free on site at TNA. Records can be searched by the year the licence was issued, the name of the convict, their estimated birth year, the court and the date of conviction. The captions are also available at TNA in hard copy, and can be requested through the catalogue.

TNA's MEPO 6 (Metropolitan Police: Criminal Record Office: Habitual Criminals Registers and Miscellaneous Papers, 1834–1959) holds details of chronic inebriates, the weekly issues of the *Police Gazette* which reported escaped and released prisoners, and the registers of habitual criminals created by the 1869 and 1871 'Habitual Offenders Acts'. The registers of all persons convicted and imprisoned for one month or more contain the name of the ex-prisoner, date and place of birth, place they served their sentence, date of discharge, length of sentence, last known address, occupation and known previous convictions. Because the registers were designed to keep track of offenders under supervision we can trace the movements of ex-prisoners as they moved in and out of London. Just as with PCOM4 the registers also contain details of appearance, and the tattoos that decorated the female convict body. These tattoos were more than embellishment, they were also a self-inscribed pictorial narrative, records women kept on their own bodies. Children's names were joined by current and past lovers, places of significance to the individual, and, sometimes, meaningful symbols (religious, gang membership, nationalistic). These can be useful to us in learning more about a criminal woman's life, loves and losses.

A more fragmentary set of records is all that is available to research another aspect of post-release supervision, the Discharged Prisoners' Aid Societies (DPAS). Although many were established, few sets of records survive. Where they do, they provide information on the practical aid that was supplied to convicts in their first few days of freedom. For example, in 1880, the Committee of the Northumberland Home for Fallen Women established a DPAS to aid prisoners after their discharge from prison by procuring suitable lodgings for such of them 'as may be selected, furnishing, temporary maintenance in case of need to individuals seeking employment, assisting them in obtaining work, or in returning to their homes and subsequently exercising a friendly supervision over them'. Their records can be found in Northumberland Archives and the Minute Book (QCDP/11850-188) reveals how they operated in the nineteenth century, whilst the Register of Female Prisoners in Receipt of Relief (QCDP/41) names the women it gave practical help to in the twentieth.

The records of South Staffordshire DPAS also illustrate something of the range of services they provided.

> Alice H. Bucknell, 31, married 2 children, C of E, Housewife. Keeping a Brothel, 3 months. Not deserving further aid, 16 pre-cons … Elizabeth Bates, 30, Single, 2 children, C of E., labourer, Neglect of Children, 6 months. Can return to former employer … Emma Burton, 49, C of E, Indecency, 1 month. Not deserving aid, she is not deserving aid, she had 4/- cash. 26 pre cons … During the month of November 1905, 38 cases have been remitted to the Society for inquiry. Aided in lodging, food, clothing, tools, rail fare. Work found for 7, restored to friends 1, re-arrested 1, entered labour home 1. Not deserving 2, no need 2.

Together these records can be used to trace prisoners inside the institution, their destination after leaving the institution, and their first few months of freedom. They offer an interesting perspective on the efforts the state made to control and observe people they thought likely to reoffend, and provide evidence for how effective those various strategies turned out to be.

ACCESSING RECORDS

The National Archives (TNA) at Kew, London, is the British government's official archive, with records dating from the Domesday Book to digital files and archived websites being stored there, available to the public. Although it is very easy to access records at Local Records Offices and Local Studies Centres, gaining access to TNA involves a few more hoops. In addition to proof of identity (and address), visitors are required to watch a short introductory video about using the catalogue, the proper handling of delicate records and so on. This ensures that the records, even those that are in

NAME and SURNAME	(1) RELATION to Head of Family—or (2) Position in the Institution.	CONDITION as to Marriage	AGE Last Birthday Male | Females	RANK, PROFESSION, or OCCUPATION	WHERE BORN	If (1) Deaf-and-Dumb (2) Blind (3) Imbecile or Idiot (4) Lunatic
1 *Lydia Lloyd*	Prisoner	Widow	39	Laundress.	Staffs. Wolverhampton	101
2 *Mary Juddow*	.	Married	45	—	Durham S. Shields	
3 *Mary Alexander*	.	Widow	44	—	Ireland.	
4 *Mary Ann Hall*	.	Widow	44	Charwoman	Yorks. Hull	
5 *Ann Evans*	.	Married	46	Ironer Laundress	Middx. Smithfield	
6 *Mary Brown*	.	Widow	33	Spinner Cotton.	Lancs. Ormskirk	
7 *Ann Wood*	.	Married	50	—	Cumberland Carlisle	
8 *Mary Ann Brown*	.	Widow	52	Laundress.	Hants. Portsmouth	
9 *Ann Fletcher*	"	Married	35	Factory operative.	Lancs. Manchester	
10 *Ellen Stevenson*	.	Married	49	Hawker	Lancs. Liverpool	

Medical notes on the caption documents for Sarah Tuff (see Chapter 25).

demand, can be preserved for future generations. Ordering is simple and easy, and normally up to four documents are produced at any one time (they take about an hour to be delivered to you).

There are now alternatives to visiting TNA in person. A selection of records is downloadable directly from the TNA website and due to licensing their holdings to commercial companies, a considerable amount of criminal justice records have been made available through commercial websites. Some records are free for anyone to access, but the majority are accessible only by paid subscription. For London's criminal women, if they were sentenced to a period of imprisonment, the lives of those individuals can be traced via the Digital Panopticon (www.digitalpanopticon.org) which has digitised a large collection of criminal and institutional records, including PCOM4 and MEPO6, and is completely free to access.

STRENGTHS AND LIMITATIONS

It is immediately apparent that records such as PCOM4 and MEPO6 hold an immense amount of data on individual prisoners and the workings of the prison and post-release systems. They contain details which are not found elsewhere for many thousands of people. We can see the daily experiences of women who were sent to convict prisons, how they survived by resisting the authorities (singing in chapel, stealing food, cheeking the warders), and what impact the prison had on their health (in the medical records). We can then see where they headed to when released from prison, who employed them and what happened to them when they infringed the conditions of their release – often they returned to prison unfortunately. The records are a great source of information normally hidden to social historians and genealogists.

Nevertheless, as with all records, they have their problems. The first is survival. Licences of parole for female convicts survive for two main periods, 1853 to 1871, and 1882 to 1887. This means that there are over four thousand available 'caption' documents to analyse, but it is unfortunate that there is a twelve-year gap meaning that crucial records are lost for hundreds of women, who just happened to fall in this date range. The second limitation is that MEPO-6 registers only refer to habitual offenders, and PCOM-4 only holds the records pertaining to convicts, leaving petty offenders, and those with few offences considerably less well documented. Only serious and repeat offenders are caught in these bureaucratic records. We lack a similarly deep and broad set of records on minor everyday offenders – who made up the vast majority of those who traipsed through the Victorian and Edwardian courts, and found themselves in a range of institutions.

We could also suggest that the information in these records needs to be linked to that found in many other records in order to provide a full and accurate picture, and last of all, we could risk the comment that there is simply too much information to process. MEPO 6 is a vast archive, containing hundreds of volumes of data; every caption document is fairly lengthy, and some are over a hundred pages long. It seems odd for researchers to complain that we have too much information, but the sheer volume of some records can considerably increase the amount of time it takes find what we are looking for.

Prison and release documents are an extraordinary set of records. They provide detailed data on heights, weights, health, prison experiences, and relationships within the convict prison that cannot be found anywhere else. PCOM4 and MEPO6 are possibly the pinnacle of prison records, and tell us much about some of the people who have been most hidden from the historian's gaze for centuries. They also allow us to follow women as they leave prison, joining together their prison lives and their existence beyond the penal estate. Prison records and release records show us how women crossed that divide, and whether they were able to make a success of their post-sentence lives, or whether they ended up going back through the revolving door of criminal justice as many did.

Chapter 39

HOW TO RESEARCH: CRIMINAL WOMEN AT HOME

Researching the lives of criminal women is not just about cataloguing their offences. What makes their stories so fascinating is not only the way in which they broke the law, but the complex personal lives that led them to do so, and the impact it had on their lives subsequently. To fully understand the nature and patterns of women's offending, we must look for evidence of the communities in which they socialised, the streets in which they worked and lived, and the kinds of residential environment they called home. While the information contained in civil records is well-known to social historians and genealogists alike, this chapter looks at how to get more from these documents, and how to read between the lines of addresses, and details of family and friends, in order to produce more considered and meaningful narratives of criminal women's lives.

KEY SOURCES

UK Census

The UK Census collection is available in a complete run from 1841 to 1911. Entries for the 1841 census (an important tool for tracing the earliest criminal women in our period) only contained limited fields of name, age (although this was often rounded to the nearest '0' or '5'), occupation, and an indication of whether the individual was born in the county or elsewhere. From 1851, however, the census followed a common administrative pattern and recorded names, ages, marital status, occupations and birthplace (except for the 1911 census which also recorded details of marriages and child mortality).

General Health previous to present imprisonment, and special maladies from which the Prisoner states he has suffered,	*never strong*	*asthma*

Census form.

The uses of the census for tracing how individuals moved around, married, had children, and worked are too well known to need much discussion here. However, as well as tracing how a woman's life was materially changing once every decade, and the evolution of their family dynamic, census entries can allow us to collect supplementary peripheral material. Keep notes of all addresses to be used in future searches, as well as the kind of residential dwelling, to learn more about the colour of life in the area, and follow up leads from prison documents which contain information about friends and family. It is surprising just how many specific streets, areas, or even particular dwellings were mentioned by social investigators in their writings. Keep lists of neighbours and those who live in the same dwelling in the case of 'lodger' women seemingly living alone, particularly men, whose surnames women often adopted as personal and criminal aliases. Ann Plowman's cohabitation with Jimmy Dodden, for example, gives us good reason to suspect that convictions for 'Ann Dodden' in the same place and time also relate to her, even though the pair were never formally married. Likewise, if we already know several aliases used by a woman from criminal records, cross-checking names with a list of neighbours from the nearest census can throw new light on relationships between seemingly unconnected people. Names of friends and neighbours might also help us identify with more certainty newspaper reports relating to criminal women – especially those with common names. Given the close proximity in which women usually lived and offended, if a victim, witness or co-offender in a newspaper shared the name of relative, boarder or neighbour, it is probably more than a coincidence. Finally, the census did not just record women at home. Many thousands of women spent census nights in institutions across Britain. When finding an institutional entry look not only at the place, name and type of institution for further research, but take note of the other inmates on the page. The average age, occupation and birthplace can give useful contextual information about the nature and purpose of the institution and how people ended up there.

Parish Records

Likewise, while we might all be familiar with searching parish records for incidents of birth, marriage and death, these records tell us about far more than the individual. For records that relate to the birth of a criminal woman's child, or her marriage, researchers would do well to take note of the names of witnesses signed at the bottom. A list of names of family and friends who agreed to act as witnesses or godparents can be essential both for future identification of an offender, and for cross-checking with reports of crime. Do close friends and family co-offend with the woman in question, or become victims of theft, violence or anti-social behaviour? Can details of the friends, family and neighbours of women be found in records of prison correspondence? If so, what does this tell us? Alternately, tracing the movement of friends and family members can also give vital clues as to what kind of support network a woman enjoyed. Though both women with supportive friends and family and those with almost no one to care for them appeared in court, the more we know about the circumstances of a woman's life, the better we can provide evidence to support, or challenge, our theories for *why* criminal women acted as they did.

To this end, records of more than just birth, marriage and death from the parish can be utilised. While convict prisons were run centrally, asylums, local prisons, workhouses, and reform homes were usually administered at the county level. Prisoners were more likely than other women to use, or be sent to, other institutions throughout their lives, and so registers of admission and discharge for a range of institutions are worth checking for traces of the women we study. Minutes from the meeting of Boards of Guardians for a particular town village or parish can also be valuable. The Guardians were those appointed to oversee welfare provision in any locality, and in meetings would regularly discuss 'problem' cases by name (for example, habitual drunks, or the severely impoverished) and make suggestions for dealing with them.

ACCESSING RECORDS

The full census collection for England and Wales is available to access for free at The National Archives. Visitors can request to view hard copies of particular enumeration districts or wards to browse, or they can choose to key-word search the census electronically for free on computers at the archive. The same digitised census material is available for a fee on online subscription sites. A transcription of the census for Scotland is available via the same online subscription sites, and in hard copy at the National Library of Scotland.

The easiest way to find relevant information in the census is of course via an electronic search. Transcription of virtually all fields makes it possible to search for women by name (including variant spellings and aliases), by other details, and even in the 1911 census by address. Keyword searches can also be valuable when it comes to finding women who were institutionalised on census night, like Amelia Layton (see Chapter 27). By using the search tool and inputting the words 'prisoner' or 'inmate' the search function will prioritise returns for personal details of those in institutions. This is not only useful for finding information about individuals, but the census can reveal the name and location of the institution they are being held in (not always specified in conviction or newspaper records), enabling researchers to focus future searches on records of that particular institution. The long-awaited 1921 census should be available to researchers in 2022, the expiration date of the widely adhered to '100 year rule'. The 1921 census contains even more personal detail on residents than previous years, and will allow us to trace criminal women right until the end of our period. Unfortunately, for those researching England and Wales, the 1921 census is likely to be the last census available to researchers for decades. A fire in 1942 completely destroyed the 1931 census (the 1931 Scottish census survives, held at the National Library of Scotland), and no census was taken during the Second World War. Thus, the next complete census was taken in 1951 and will not be available until approximately 2052.

While online subscription sites have invested a great deal of time and money in digitising parish records of birth, marriage and death for a number of locations around the UK, local archives remain one of the best places to search for civil information relating to criminal women – particularly petty offenders confined in local prisons or reform homes. Most local archives will hold parish registers of birth, marriage and death for the majority of our period. However, these will usually be in hard copy only and so cannot be name searched. Details of the type of event and the year in which it took place, as well as the parish (for big towns and cities) must be known before specific volumes and relevant pages can be provided. Online search facilities such as FreeBMD, though limited, can be useful in obtaining this information before a trip to the record office. Local archives will also usually contain prison registers for the area, workhouse, reformatory and other charitable institution records as well as parish guardian minutes, and the local census records. When trying to identify exactly what the local archives or local studies centre does contain, you can start with the online catalogues which give useful details of the collection, and, if further questions remain, contacting local archivists is often the most direct way of resolving a query about the availability of any particular record set.

STRENGTHS AND LIMITATIONS

The better the information we collect about criminal women, the easier it is for us to locate them in a range of diverse records in which they left a trace. Civil records, particularly those from early life, can give us the best sense of personal details like age and birthplace which often become contradictory in later documents. Information on occupations, friends and family and personal relationships can help us identify convicts in newspaper reports, letters and criminal records, create timelines for their lives and movements, and add vital context to the tales we tell of their offending. Parish records are essential for finding out more about the place and time in which the women we seek lived, and can provide vital clues to what life was like for them both inside and outside a range of institutions.

Sometimes, no matter how diligently we search, the individuals we seek simply did not leave enough evidence to be found. Those women that regularly changed address, or did not have close family or friendship support networks, fell through the cracks of official record collection. Those living the most precarious lives, staying in common lodging houses and finding themselves regularly in and out of institutions, often the very women we seek, were in many cases actively trying not to be found. It was not unknown for individuals to try to refuse to answer a census enumerator's questions, or to give false and conflicting details of themselves. We must always remember that many of the criminal women we research had a long-standing and understandable mistrust of authority. That is to say nothing of the human errors and administrative slips that leave women who were actually registered in the census or parish records under wrong or misspelt names, making them virtually impossible for us to find.

We must also accept that, despite enthusiastic investigation by sociologists, philanthropists, and the great and the good of Britain's many towns and cities, the picture they paint of any location does not represent a universal experience. Even the most exclusive residential areas were in close proximity to dens of crime and vice, and even in the lowest streets full of common lodging houses were home to women trying to earn an honest living.

Reading between the lines of civil records, and taking note of incidental details can be an important step in tracing a criminal woman's story and bringing it to life. Knowing more about the streets in which they lived, the milestones in their lives, and the other people with which they had significant connections can help us trace them in other sources, and assist us in distinguishing commonly named convicts from others who share their names. Civil records can help explain the personal circumstances which led to offending and give vital contextual clues to why offenders acting as they did, from the crimes they became embroiled in, to the choice of their aliases. Understanding more about the world in which they lived, and the multiple struggles women could face in their daily lives leave us better equipped to interpret and tell their stories.

Chapter 40

CONCLUSION

Some of the most interesting journeys begin in a library. We have tried to provide a guide which allows you to follow through the women you are interested in as they move in and out (and sometimes in again!) of various prisons, and other carceral and semi-carceral institutions.

Here we have tried to enthuse and interest you, by providing you with stories about convict women, girls in reformatories, inebriates, criminal lunatics and women packed onto convict vessels and sent to Van Diemen's Land: individuals all lumped together by society and the justice system as 'criminal women'. The women whose stories we tell in this book are not representative of *all* incarcerated women. We have revealed the stories of two women who were executed – Amelia Sach and Emily Swann – a twentieth of our sample of stories, but few women were actually executed in this period, certainly far fewer than one in twenty of convicted women. We also have stories from Broadmoor, Britain's first home for the criminally insane. Although approximately a quarter of the inmates there were female, there were only about three hundred women there at any one time, whilst there were thousands in local and convict prison. Most 'offending' women were in and out of local prisons serving sentences for drunkenness and petty theft. We have stories of women who were repeatedly imprisoned on short sentences too, of course, but if we wanted to be representative almost every case study would feature local prisoners. So why have we not done that? We have tried to show the richness of the sources we can find on 'criminal' women, and also to show the range of institutions that contained women in this period, but mainly because one's own ancestors never neatly fall into representative groups. Few family historians have ancestors who were executed, but their stories tell us much about women who suffered the most terrible of sentences. Again, the Broadmoor inmates made up only a tiny percentage of incarcerated women, but they reveal much about the treatment of women who suffered from post-natal depression. Women who were repeatedly locked up in local prisons show us how repeat incarceration interrupted some women's lives to the point when they became indigent, whilst other women managed their repeated short prison sentences within family life and employment careers. The women we portray were representative of some things, but had unique experiences nonetheless. That is what, perhaps, makes their stories interesting to read.

Some of the women who broke the law in the nineteenth and twentieth centuries spent months or years languishing in local or convict prisons, some travelled halfway around the world, being transported from friends and family to new lives. The crimes they committed would generally not merit prison sentences today, though some would, for women were as capable of committing serious crimes as men. Infanticide, however, and prostitution, were labelled as particularly female crimes (despite the vast majority of women sentenced to prison being convicted of minor thefts and challenges to public order). Women too experienced punishments that were not imposed as much on men – being sent to a female inebriates home for example, so that they could relearn how to be 'proper women'. Men seldom had to learn how to be more 'manly' in prisons (although standing up for oneself and being physically strong was a great help) but women had to learn how to adhere to dominant views of femininity. This was the case in the inebriates homes but it was also the case in prisons, where offending women who swore, were obscene, were loud or were troublesome were all punished for not acting in the demure, respectable and peaceful 'womanly' manner that Victorian society demanded.

If the demands on offending women in prison have somewhat lessened today, echoing societal norms about femininity, other things have not. Women then as now were separated from their loved ones when they were 'sent down', and they were separated from their children. Few can understand how that would have felt, nor can we ever fully experience the pains of imprisonment for those poor women. We can go to the prisons within which they were confined, with many of the places of confinement now open to the public. These places provide us with a sense of the physical space that women were kept in, which archives cannot; we can see how small the cells were, we can feel the thinness of the mattresses that women slept on. We can rub our hands over the rough walls, and imagine what it was like to have every minute of the day ordered by an unyielding prison timetable day after day, for years.

Your genealogical journey to find one or any number of criminal women may have started in a library, by viewing an online website, or maybe even with this book, but it is unlikely to end there. If we have helped to further increase your interest in women's lives or in the history of crime, there are other texts we recommend you take a look at (ones we ourselves have used in our research and in writing this book, and others that provide useful information about prisons, the period and lives of women at this time). Few genealogical and historical journeys are linear – they seldom go direct from A to B as we know. Some journeys are circular, many take numerous twists and turns before arriving at an end point (although end points are few and far between, most are just the start of a new journey of enquiry). We hope that we have given you a reasonable map that will help you when you make your own journeys to trace a range of curious, confounding, and above all, fascinating, criminal women.

FURTHER READING

Contemporary Writings

Acton, W, *Prostitution Considered in its Moral, Social, and Sanitary Aspects* (London: John Churchill, 1857).

Booth, C, *Labour and Life of the People* (London: Williams & Norgate, 1891).

Booth, W, *In Darkest England, and the Way Out* (London: Salvation Army, 1890).

Engels, F, *The Condition of the Working Class in England in 1844* (London: S. Sonnenschein, 1892).

Maybrick, F, *Mrs Maybrick's Own Story: My Fifteen Lost Years* (London: Funk & Wagnalls Co., 1905).

Mayhew, H, *London Labour and the London Poor*, vol. 4 (London, 1861).

Mayhew, H, and Binney, J, *The Criminal Prisons of London and Scenes of Prison Life* (London: Frank Cass, 1968 edition).

London, J, *The People of the Abyss* (London, 1903).

Modern Histories

Brodie, A, Croom, J, and Davies, J, *English Prisons: An Architectural History* (London: English Heritage, 2002).

Cox, P, *Gender, Justice and Welfare: Bad Girls in Britain, 1900–1950* (Basingstoke: Palgrave Macmillan, 2003).

Forsythe, W, *The Reform of Prisoners 1830–1900* (London: Croom Helm, 1987).

Godfrey, B, Cox, D, and Farrall, S, *Criminal Lives: Family, Employment and Offending* (Clarendon Series in Criminology, Oxford: Oxford University Press, 2007).

Gray, D, *Crime Policing and Punishment in England 1660–1914* (London: Bloomsbury, 2016).

Griffiths, A, *Memorials of Millbank and Chapters in Prison History*, vol. 1 (London: Elibron Classics, 1875/2005).

Hartman, M, *Victorian Murderesses: A True History of Thirteen Respectable French and English Women Accused of Unspeakable Crimes* (London: Robson Books, 1985).

Higgs, M, *Prison Life in Victorian England* (Stroud: Tempus, 2007).

Johnston, H, *Crime in England 1815–1880: Experiencing the Criminal Justice System* (London: Routledge, 2015).

Johnston, H, Cox, D, and Godfrey, B, *100 Convicts: Life Inside and Outside of Prison* (Barnsley: Pen and Sword, 2016).

Johnston, H, Godfrey, B, Cox, D, and Turner, J, 'Reconstructing Prison Lives: Criminal Lives in the Digital Age', *Prison Services Journal*, 2013, Special Edition 'The Prison and the Public'.

McConville, S, *A History of English Prison Administration*, vol. 1, 1750–1877 (London: Routledge & Kegan Paul, 1995).

Oxley, D, *Convict Maids: The Forced Migration of Women to Australia* (Cambridge: Cambridge University Press, 1996).

Priestley, P, *Victorian Prison Lives: English Prison Biography, 1830–1914* (London: Pimlico, 1999).

Williams, L, *Wayward Women: Female Offending in Victorian England* (Barnsley: Pen and Sword, 2016).

Zedner, L, *Women, Crime and Custody in Victorian England* (Oxford: Oxford University Press, 1991).

Zedner, L, 'Wayward Sisters: The Prison for Women', in M Norval and D Rothman (eds), *The Oxford History of the Prison: The Practice of Punishment in Western Society* (Oxford: Oxford University Press, 1995).

INDEX